Central Music

5038 N. Central
Phoenix, AZ 85012
(602) 274-6532
(602) 274-1149 FAX

George Harrison Anthology

RECORDED VERSIONS GUITAR

AUTHENTIC TRANSCRIPTIONS
NOTES AND TABLATURE

CONTENTS

5 ALL THINGS MUST PASS

10 ALL THOSE YEARS AGO

16 APPLE SCRUFFS

21 BADGE

26 BANGLA DESH

32 BLOW AWAY

37 CRACKERBOX PALACE

44 DARK HORSE

48 FOR YOU BLUE

52 GIVE ME LOVE (GIVE ME PEACE ON EARTH)

60 HERE COMES THE SUN

64 I ME MINE

69 ISN'T IT A PITY

74 MY SWEET LORD

78 PIGGIES

82 SAVOY TRUFFLE

86 SOMETHING

90 THIS SONG

94 WAH WAH

104 WAKE UP MY LOVE

112 WHAT IS LIFE

128 WHEN WE WAS FAB

116 WHILE MY GUITAR GENTLY WEEPS

124 YOU

135 NOTATION LEGEND

Transcribed by KENN CHIPKIN, ALEX HOUTON, DANNY BEGELMAN & DAN SEIDEN

ISBN 0-7935-1088-0

Hal Leonard Publishing Corporation

7777 West Bluemound Road P.O. Box 13819 Milwaukee, WI 53213

All Things Must Pass

By George Harrison

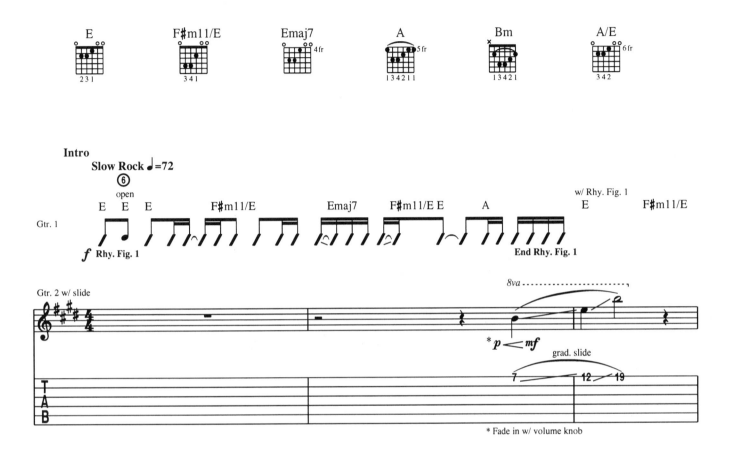

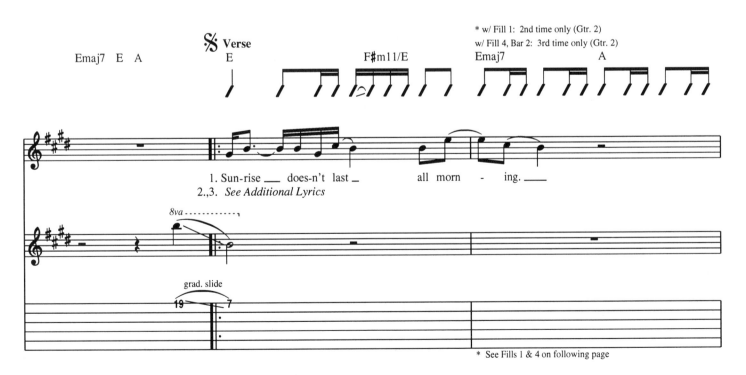

* See Fills 1 & 4 on following page

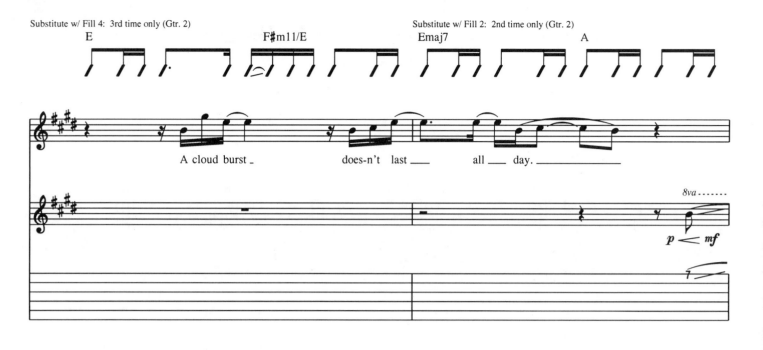

A cloud burst _ does-n't last __ all __ day. _____

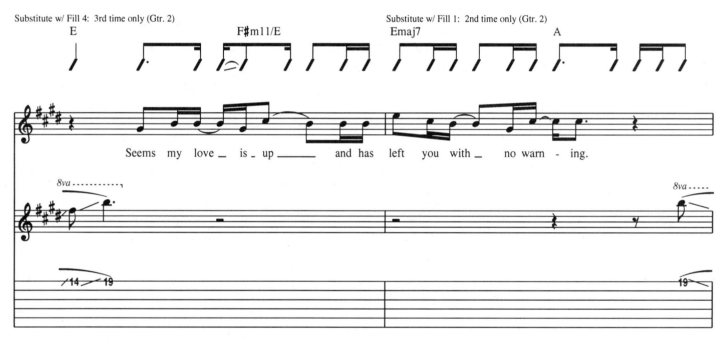

Seems my love _ is _ up _____ and has left you with _ no warn - ing.

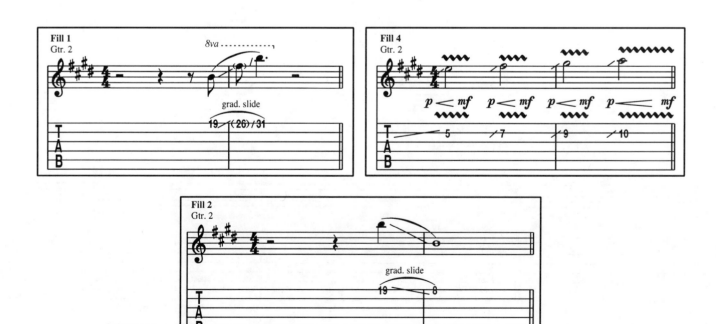

⊕ *Coda*

Additional Lyrics

Verse 2

Sunset doesn't last all evening.
A mind can blow those clouds away.
After all this, my love is up and must be leaving.
It's not always gonna be this grey.

Verse 3

The darkness only stays the night time.
In the morning it will fade away.
Daylight is good at arriving at the right time.
It's not always gonna be this grey.

All Those Years Ago

By George Harrison

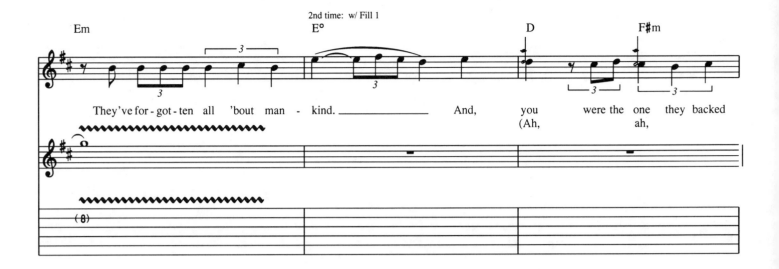

They've for-got-ten all 'bout man-kind. _____ And, you were the one they backed
(Ah, ah,

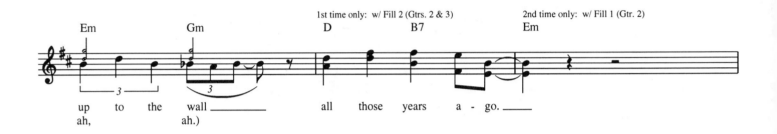

up to the wall _____ all those years a - go. _____
ah, ah.)

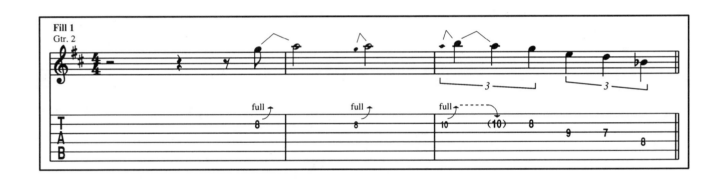

Fill 1
Gtr. 2

Fill 2
Gtr. 2
Gtr. 3

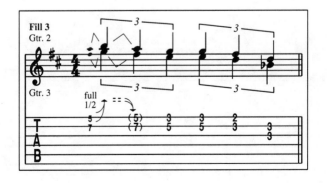

Fill 3
Gtr. 2
Gtr. 3

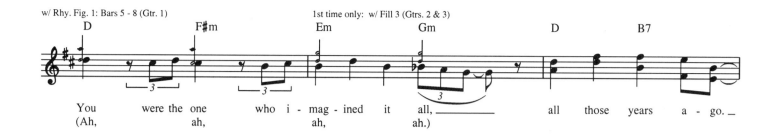

w/ Rhy. Fig. 1: Bars 5 - 8 (Gtr. 1)   1st time only: w/ Fill 3 (Gtrs. 2 & 3)

You were the one who i-mag-ined it all, _____ all those years a-go. __
(Ah,   ah,   ah,   ah.)

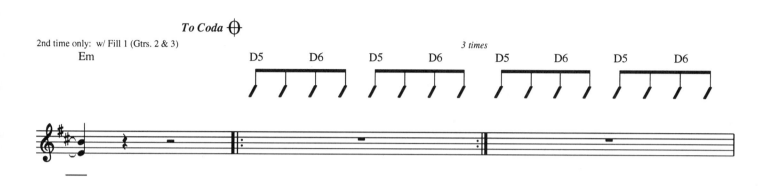

To Coda ⊕

2nd time only: w/ Fill 1 (Gtrs. 2 & 3)

3 times

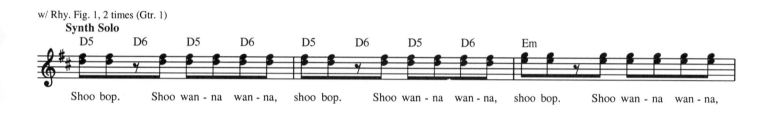

w/ Rhy. Fig. 1, 2 times (Gtr. 1)

Synth Solo

Shoo bop.   Shoo wan - na wan - na, shoo bop.   Shoo wan - na wan - na, shoo bop.   Shoo wan - na wan - na,

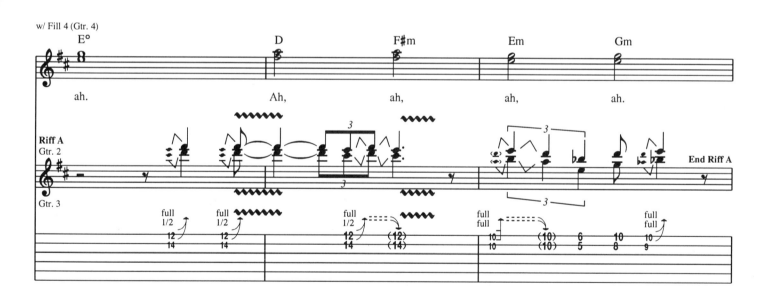

w/ Fill 4 (Gtr. 4)

ah.   Ah,   ah,   ah,   ah.

Riff A
Gtr. 2

End Riff A

Gtr. 3

full   full
1/2   1/2   full   full   full
12   12   12   (12)   10   (10) 6   10   10
14   14   14   (14)   10   (10) 5   8   9

Fill 4
Gtr. 4

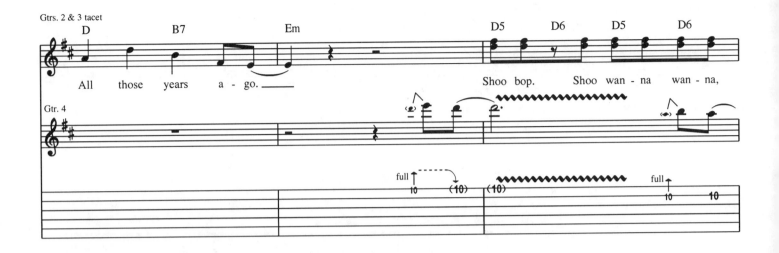

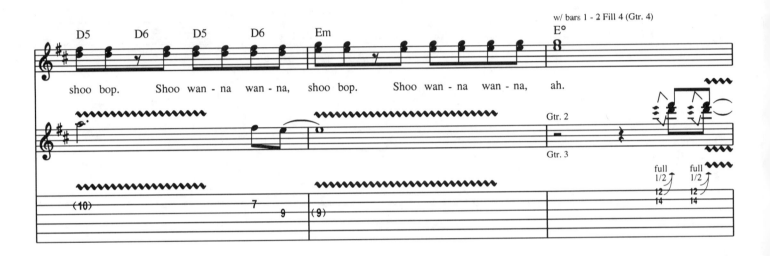

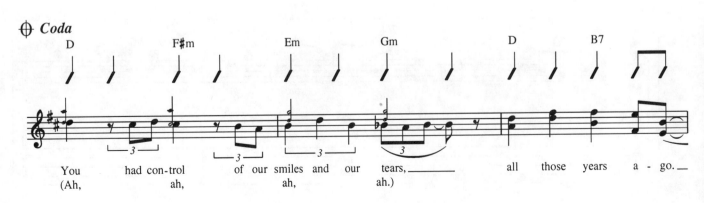

Additional Lyrics

Bridge 2

Deep in the darkest night,
I send out a prayer to you,
Now in the world of light
Where the spirit free of the lies
And all else that we despised.

Verse 4

They've forgotten all about God;
He's the only reason we exist.
Yet you were the one that they
Said was so weird,
All those years ago.
You said it all, though not
Many had ears,
All those years ago.

Apple Scruffs

By George Harrison

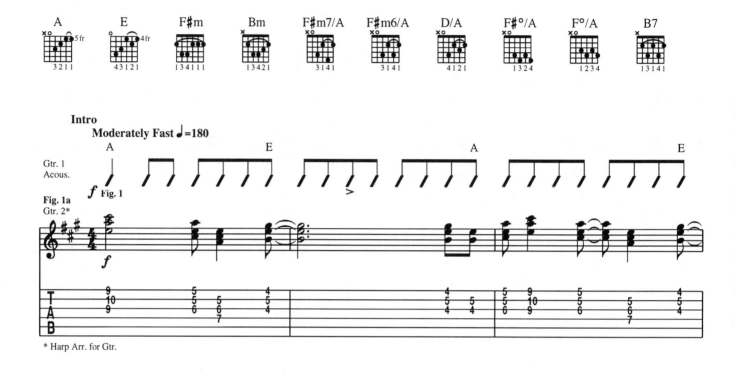

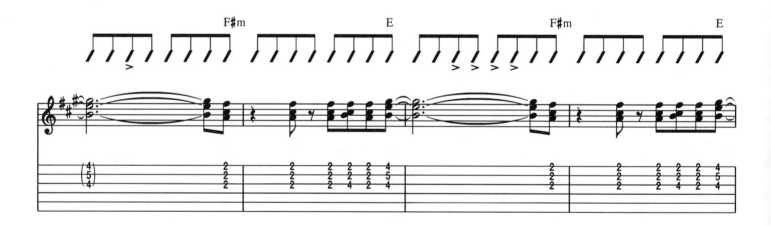

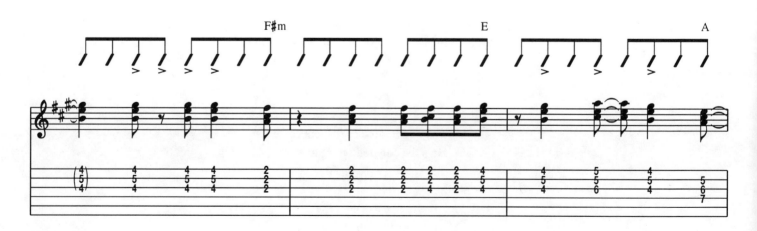

how I love ___ you,   how I love

w/ Rhy. Figs. 1 & 1a:
Bars 1 - 10 (Gtrs. 1 & 2)
Bridge

End Rhy. Fig. 2

___ you.

w/ Rhy. Figs. 1 & 1a: Bars 11 - 14

D.S. al Coda

3. In   the   fog ___

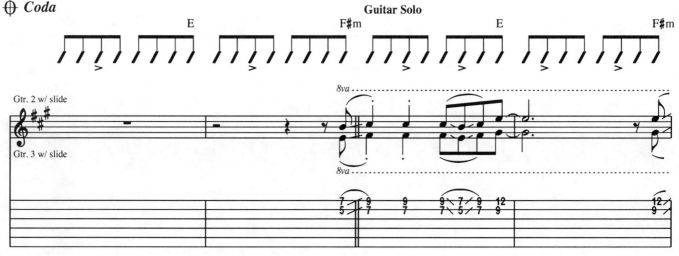

⊕ *Coda*

Guitar Solo

Gtr. 2 w/ slide
Gtr. 3 w/ slide

Additional Lyrics

Verse 2

You've been stood around for years,
Seen my smile and touched my tears,
Now it's been a long, long time
And how you've been on my mind, my apple scruffs.

Verse 3

In the fog and in the rain,
Through the pleasures and the pain,
On the step outside you stand
With your flowers in your hand, my apple scruffs.

Verse 4

While the years, they come and go
Now your love must surely show,
That beyond all time and space
We're together face to face, my apple scruffs.

Badge

Words and Music by Eric Clapton and George Harrison

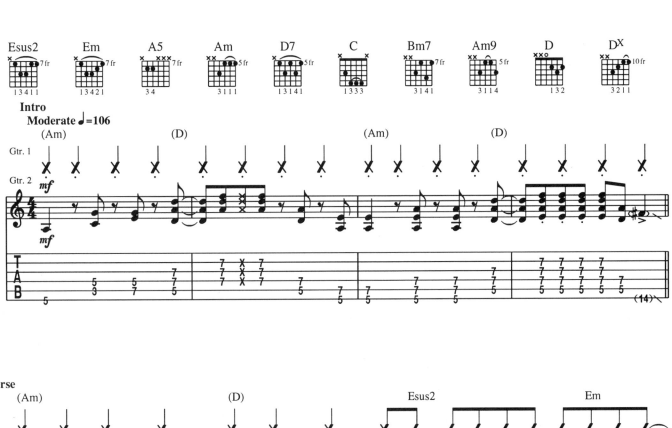

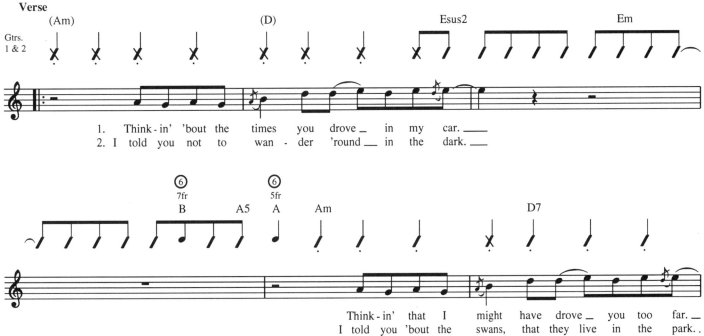

1. Think-in' 'bout the times you drove __ in my car. __
2. I told you not to wan-der 'round __ in the dark. __

Think-in' that I might have drove __ you too far. __
I told you 'bout the swans, that they live in the park. .

Substitute w/ Rhy. Fill 1: 2nd time (Gtr. 2)

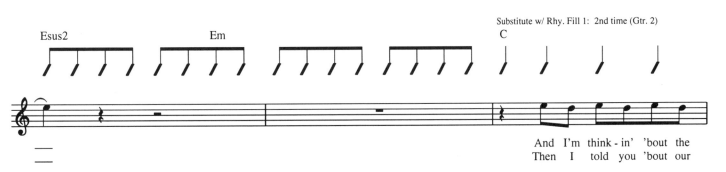

And I'm think-in' 'bout the
Then I told you 'bout our

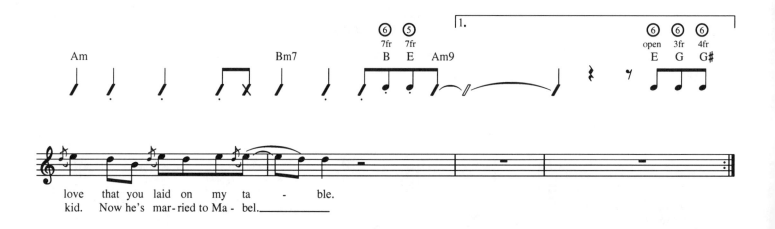

love that you laid on my ta - ble.
kid. Now he's mar-ried to Ma - bel.

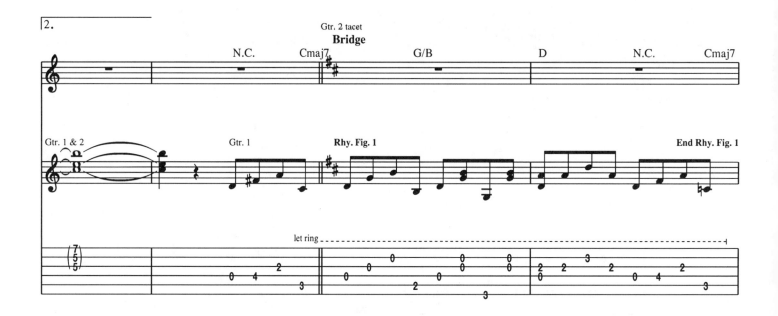

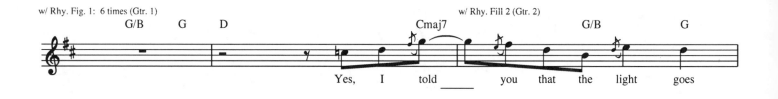

Yes, I told ____ you that the light goes

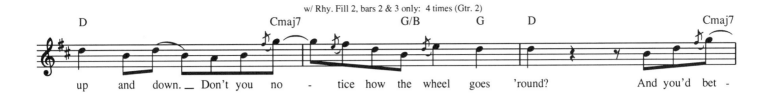

up and down.__ Don't you no - tice how the wheel goes 'round? And you'd bet -

- ter pick your - self up from the ground, __ be - fore __ they bring the cur - tain down.__

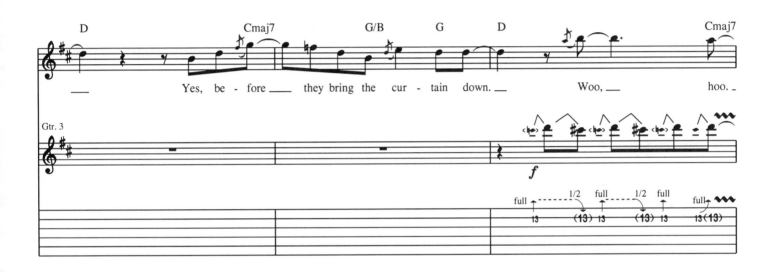

- __ Yes, be - fore __ they bring the cur - tain down. __ Woo, __ hoo. _

w/ Rhy. Fig. 1: 6 times (Gtrs. 1 & 2)

Guitar Solo

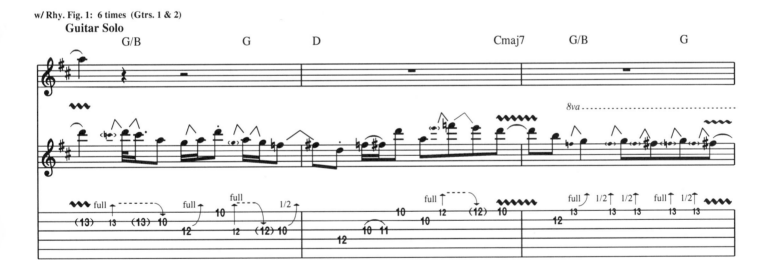

23

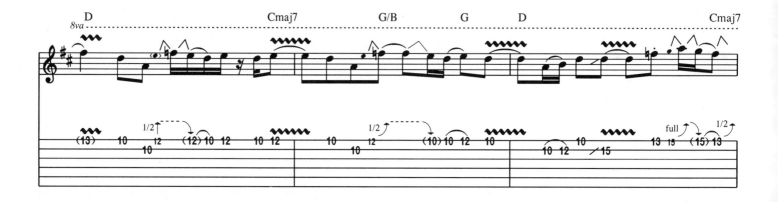

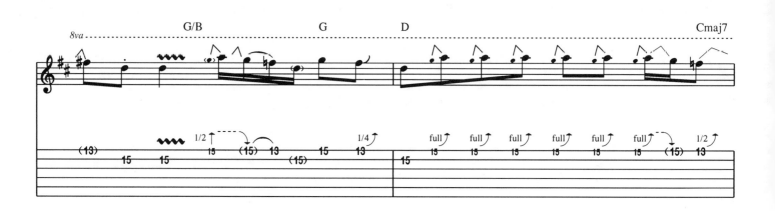

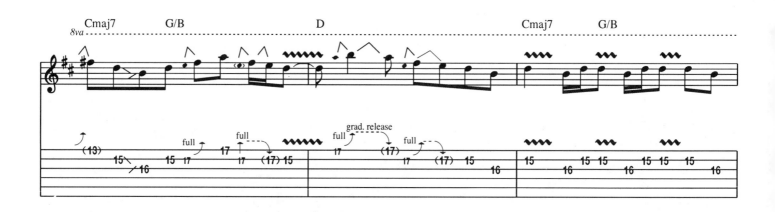

Bangla Desh

By George Harrison

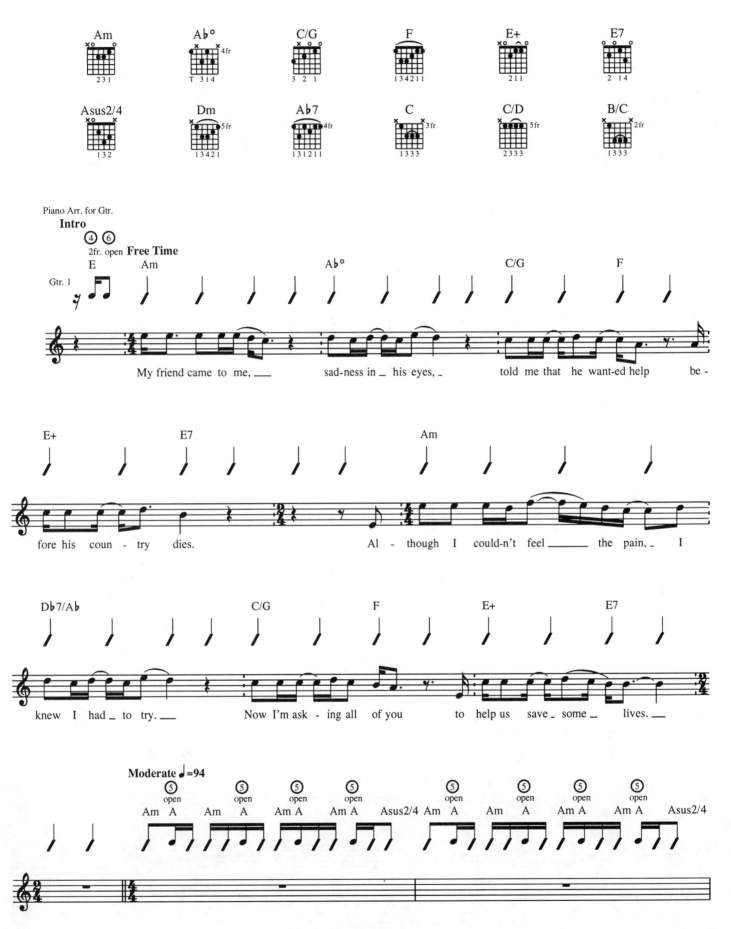

lend your __ hand; __ try to un - der - stand; __ re - lieve the peo - ple __ of Ban - gla

1.

2.

D.S. al Coda

End Rhy. Fig. 2

Desh.

Desh. __

let ring

w/ Rhy. Fig. 1 (Gtr. 1)
Piano Solo

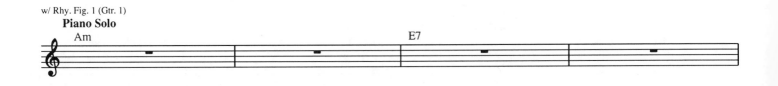

w/ Rhy. Fig. 2 (Gtr. 1)
Saxophone Solo

Gtr. 3 *

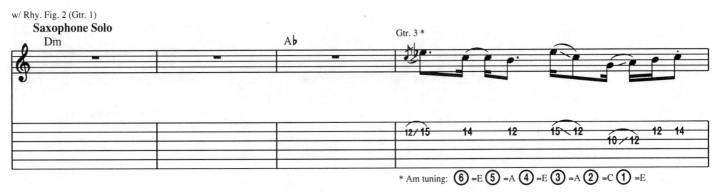

* Am tuning: ⑥ =E ⑤ =A ④ =E ③ =A ② =C ① =E

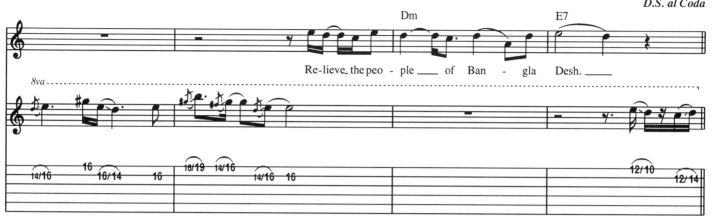

Dm E7

Re-lieve the peo - ple ___ of Ban - gla Desh. ___

Coda

Gtr. 1

C C/D C C/B C E7

Desh. _ Re-lieve the peo -

Dm C C/D C C/B C E7

ple ___ of Ban - gla Desh. ___

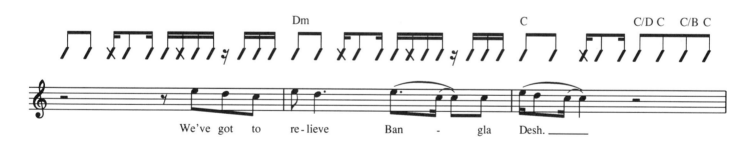

Dm C C/D C C/B C

We've got to re-lieve Ban - gla Desh. ___

w/Rhy. Fig. 1 (Gtr. 1)

Am E7

Mmm. ___ Mmm. ___

Gtr. 3

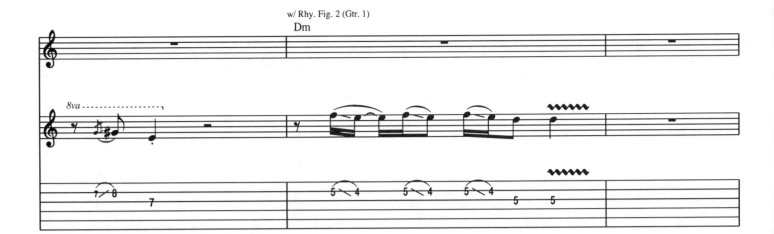

Now won't __ you   lend   your   hand _____   and

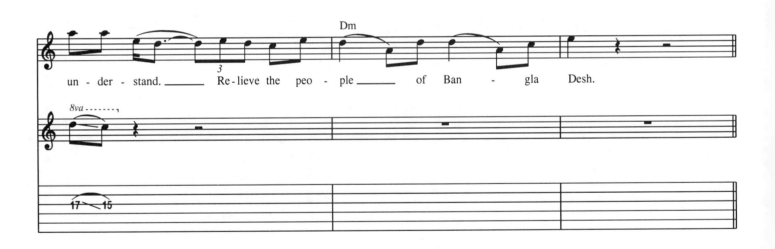

un - der - stand. _____ Re - lieve the peo - ple _____ of Ban - gla Desh.

30

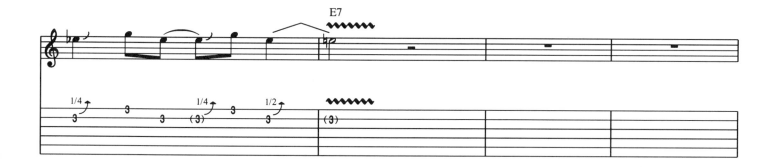

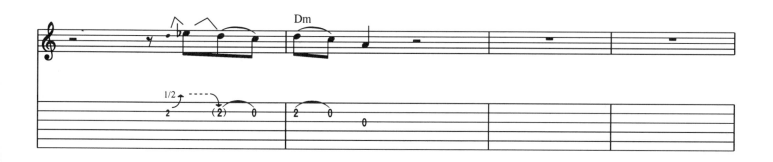

Fade

Additional Lyrics

Verse 2

Bangla Desh, Bangla Desh,
Such a great disaster, I don't understand,
But it sure looks like a mess.
I've never known such distress.
Now please don't turn away.
I wanna hear you say,
"Relieve the people of Bangla Desh."

Verse 3

Bangla Desh, Bangla Desh,
Now it may seem so far from where we all are.
It's something we can't reject.
The suff'ring I can't neglect.
Now won't you give some bread?
Get the starving fed.
We've got to relieve Bangla Desh.

Blow Away

By George Harrison

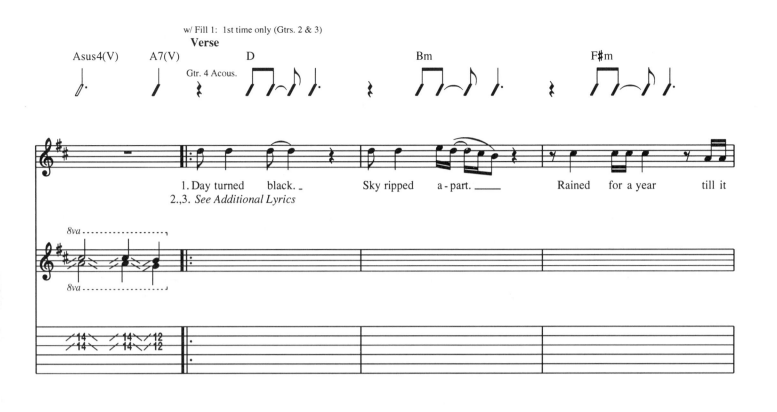

w/ Fill 1: 1st time only (Gtrs. 2 & 3)

Verse

1. Day turned black. Sky ripped a-part. Rained for a year till it

2.,3. *See Additional Lyrics*

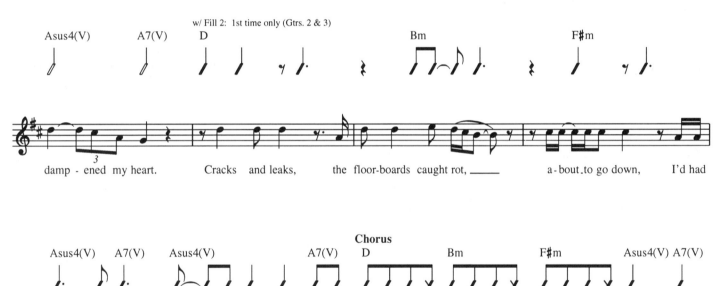

w/ Fill 2: 1st time only (Gtrs. 2 & 3)

damp-ened my heart. Cracks and leaks, the floor-boards caught rot, a-bout to go down, I'd had

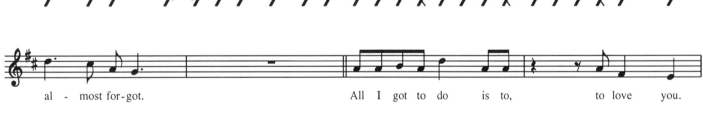

Chorus

al - most for-got. All I got to do is to, to love you.

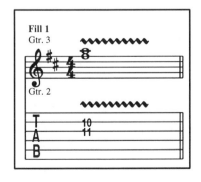

Fill 1
Gtr. 3
Gtr. 2

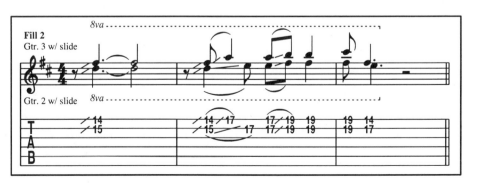

Fill 2
Gtr. 3 w/ slide
Gtr. 2 w/ slide

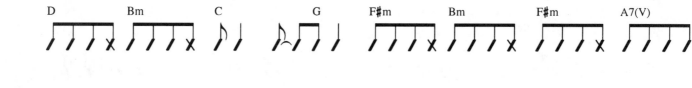

All I got to be is ___ be hap - py. All it's got to take is some warmth to make_ it blow a -

way, blow a - way, ___ blow a - way. All I got to do is to, to love you.

All I got to be is ___ be hap - py. All it's got to take is some warmth to make_ it blow a -

way, blow a - way, ___ blow a - way.

Interlude

Riff A

End Riff A

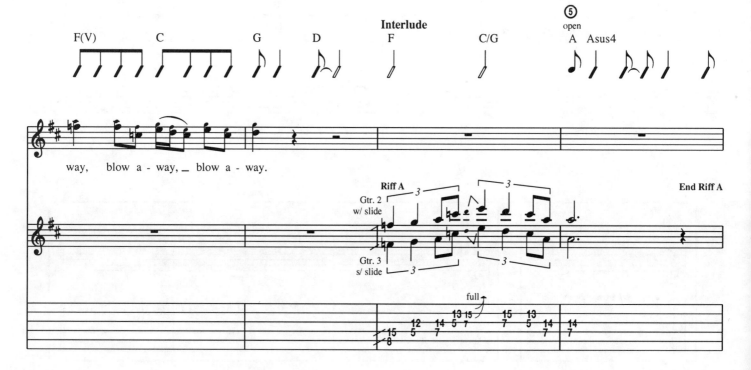

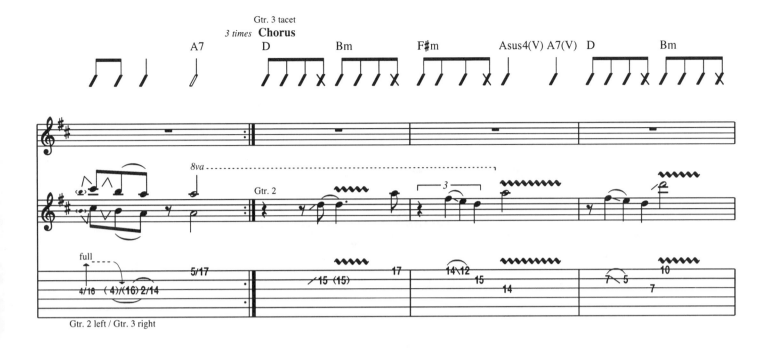

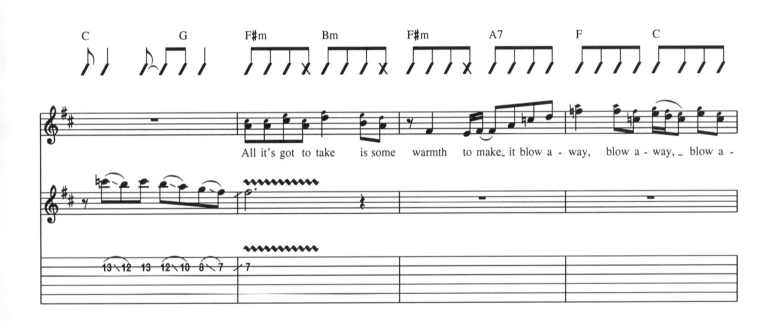

All it's got to take   is some   warmth   to make it blow a - way,   blow a - way, _ blow a -

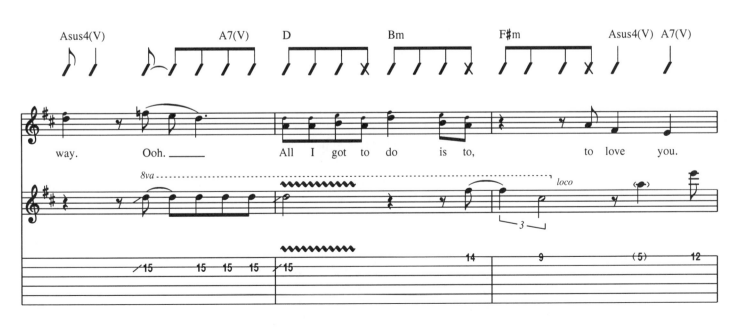

way.   Ooh. _____   All I got to do   is to,   to love you.

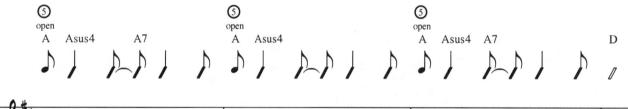

Additional Lyrics

Verse 2

Sky cleared up, day turned to bright.
Closing both eyes, now the head filled with light.
Hard to remember the state I was in,
Instant amnesia, yang to the yin.

Verse 3

Wind blew in, cloud was dispersed.
Rainbows appearing, the pressures were burst.
Breezes a-singing, now feeling good.
The moment had passed like I knew that it should.

Crackerbox Palace

By George Harrison

1. I was so young when I was born,⸺ my eyes could not yet see.⸺
2.,3. *See Additional Lyrics*

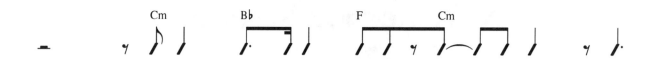

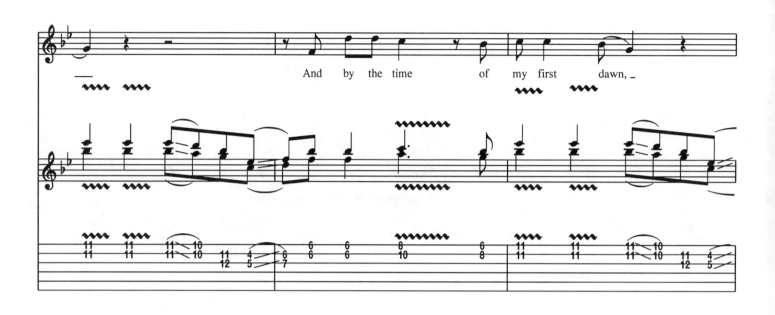

And by the time of my first dawn, _

w/ Fill 1 (Gtr. 2)
Chorus

some-bod-y hold - ing me, ____ they said, "I wel-come you ____ to Crack-er-box Pal-ace.

End Riff A   Rhy. Fig. 1
Gtr.4

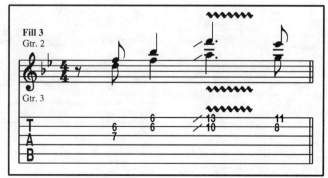

Fill 3
Gtr. 2

Gtr. 3

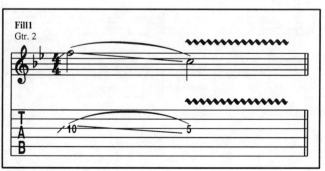

Fill1
Gtr. 2

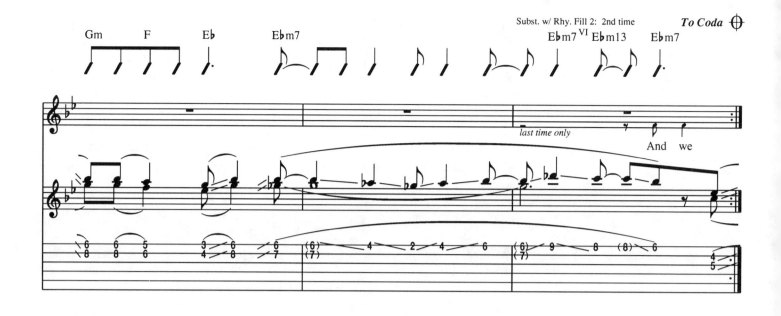

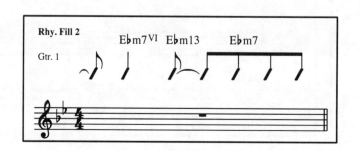

You bring such joy to Crack-er-box Pal-ace. No __ mat-ter where you roam, know our love _ is true."_

"It's true.   It's true."

D.S. al Coda

⊕ *Coda*

wel-come you _ to Crack-er-box Pal-ace.   We've been ex-pect-ing you. ____

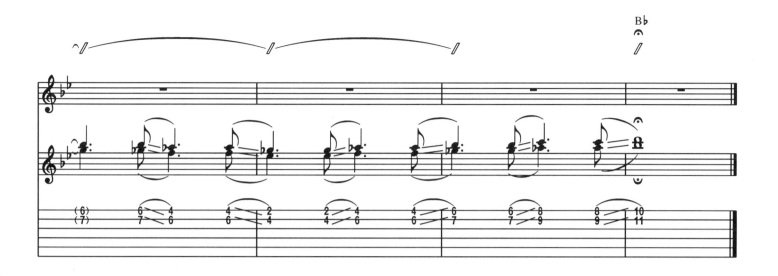

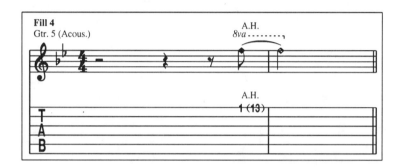

Additional Lyrics

Verse 2

While growing up or trying to,
Not knowing where to start,
I looked around for someone who
May help reveal my heart. Someone said,

Chorus 2

"While you're a part of Crackerbox Palace
Do what the rest all do,
Or face the fact that Crackerbox Palace
May have no other choice than to deport you."

Verse 3

Some times are good, some times are bad.
That's all a part of life.
And standing in between them all,
I met a Mr. Grief. And he said,

Chorus 3

"I welcome you to Crackerbox Palace,
Was not expecting you.
Let's rap and tap at Crackerbox Palace.
Know that the the Lord is well and inside of you."

Dark Horse

By George Harrison

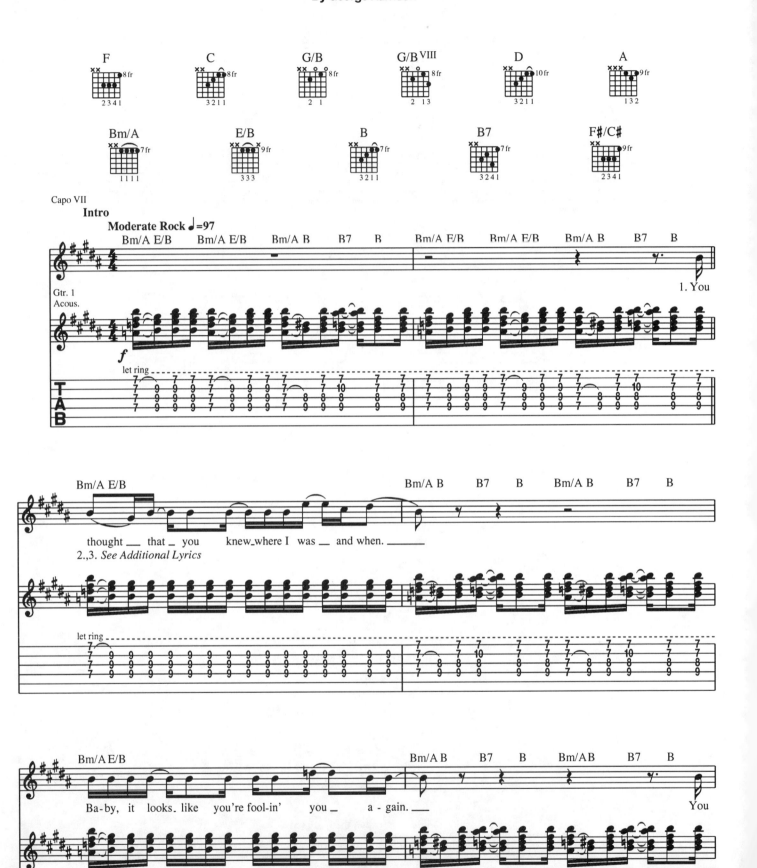

Additional Lyrics

Verse 2

You thought that you'd got me in your grip.
Baby, looks like you was not so smart.
And I became too slippery for you,
But let me tell you that was nothin' new.

Verse 3

I thought that you knew it all along,
Until you started getting me not right.
Seems as if you heard a little late.
I warned you when we both was at the startin' gate.

For You Blue

By George Harrison

49

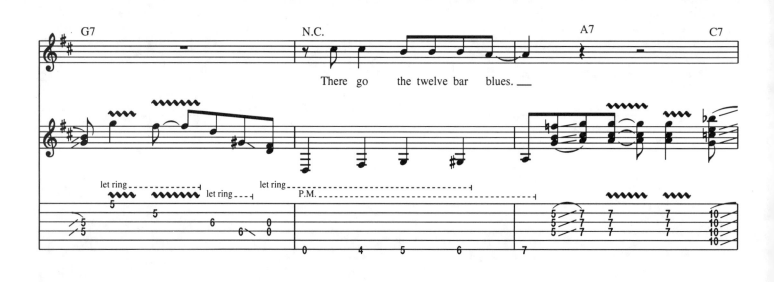

Piano Solo

El-more James_ got noth-in' on this ba-by!

D.S. al Coda

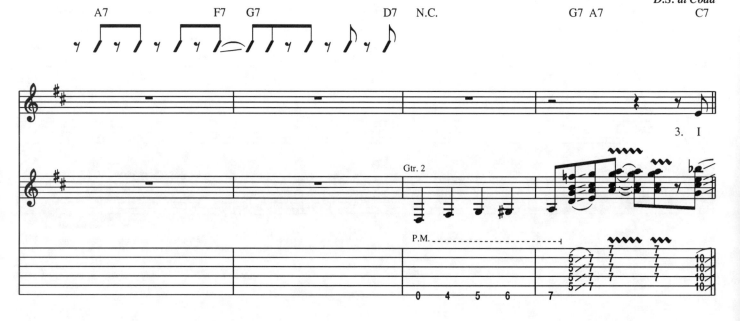

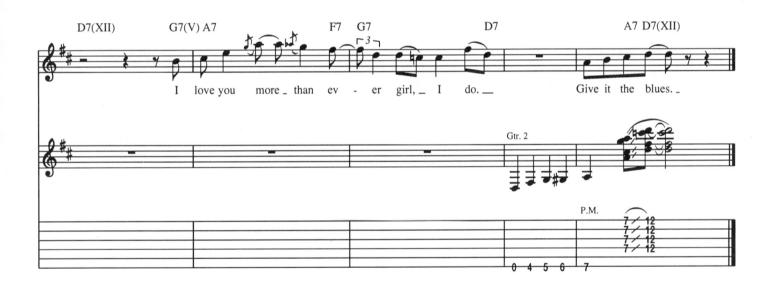

Additional Lyrics

Verse 2

I want you in the morning girl.
I love you.
I want you at the moment I feel blue.
I'm living every moment girl, for you.

Verse 3

I loved you from the moment
I saw you.
You looked at me, that's all you had to do.
I feel it now, I hope you feel it too.

Give Me Love
(Give Me Peace On Earth)

By George Harrison

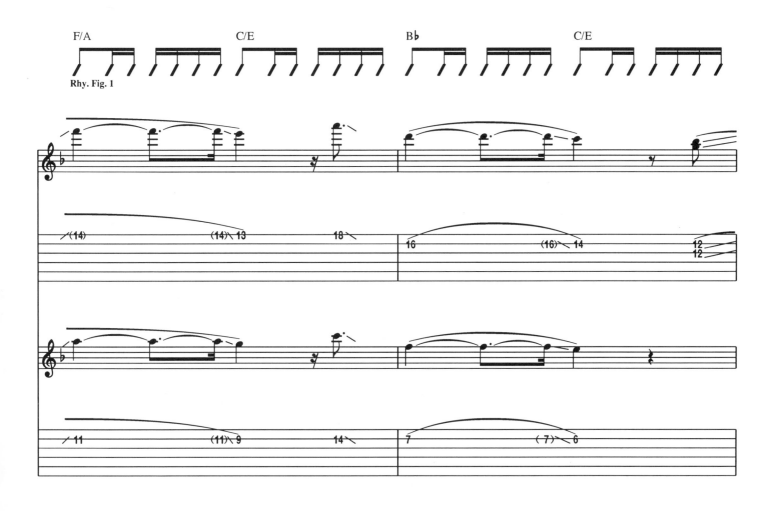

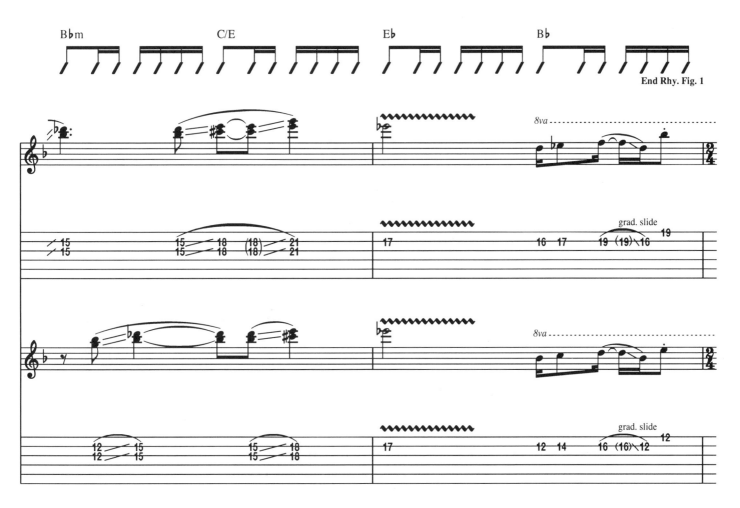

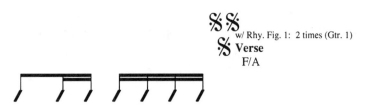

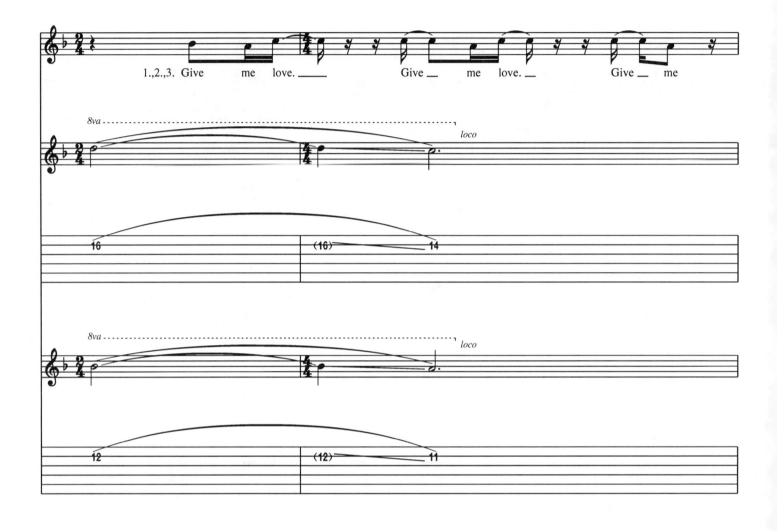

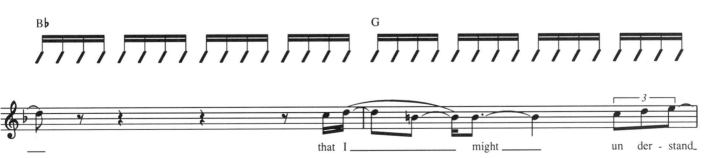

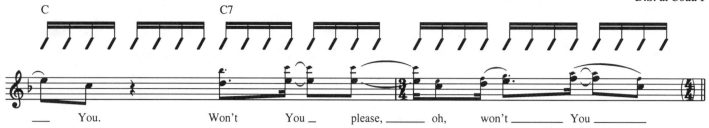

You. Won't You please, oh, won't You

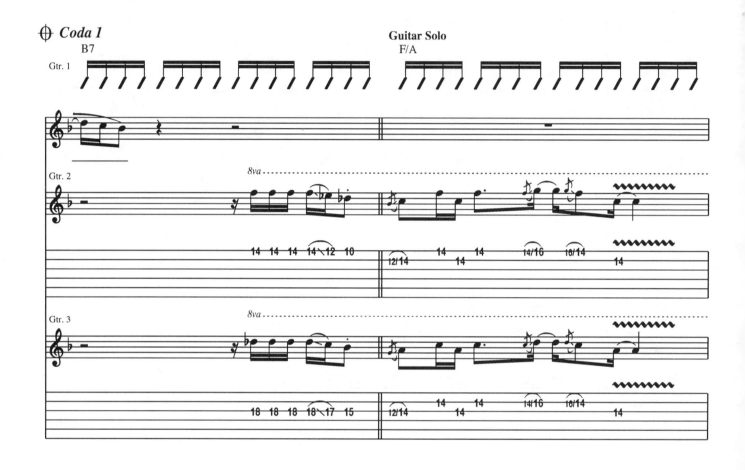

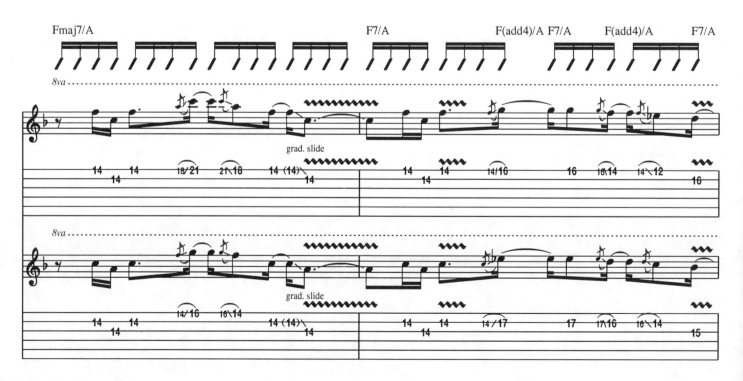

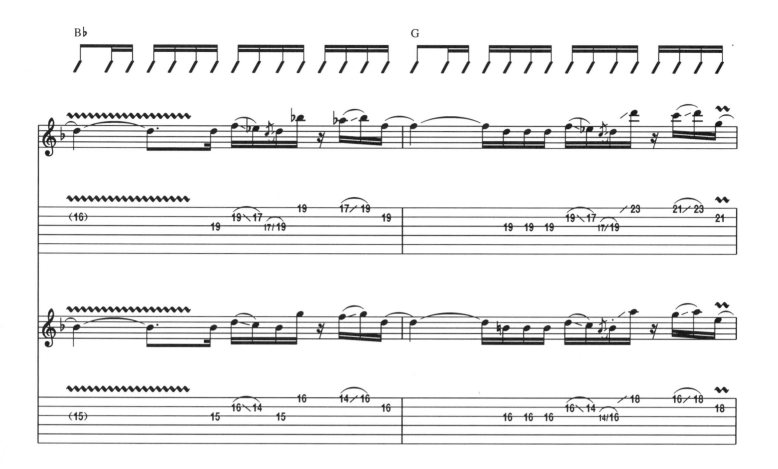

D.S.S. al Coda 2

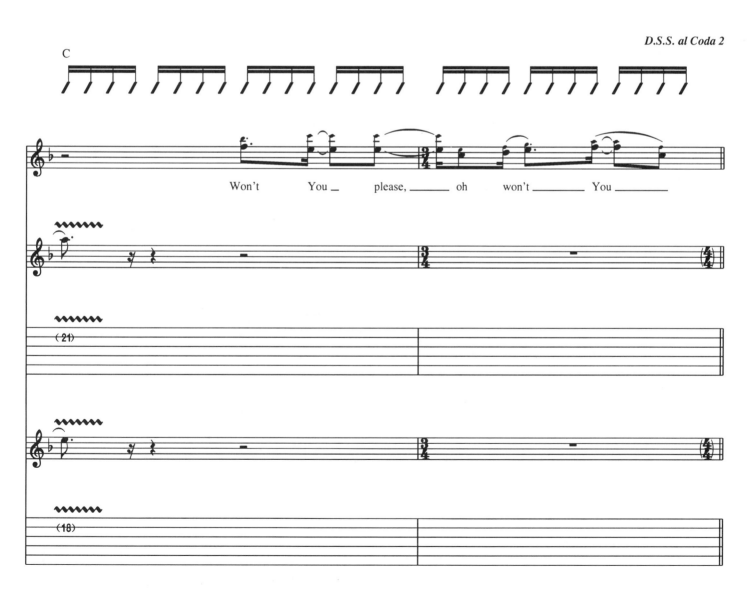

Won't   You __ please, _____ oh   won't _____ You _____

Coda 2

w/ Rhy. Fig. 1 (Gtr. 1)

Give me love. Give me love. Give me peace on earth. Give me light.

Give me life. Keep me, keep me free from birth. Now give

w/ Rhy. Fig. 1: Bars 1 & 2 (Gtr. 1)

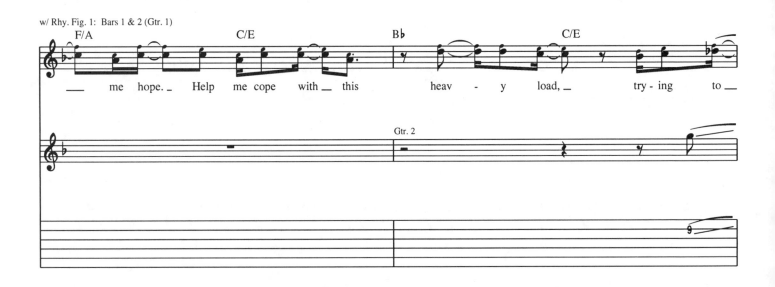

me hope. Help me cope with this heav-y load, try-ing to

Gtr. 2

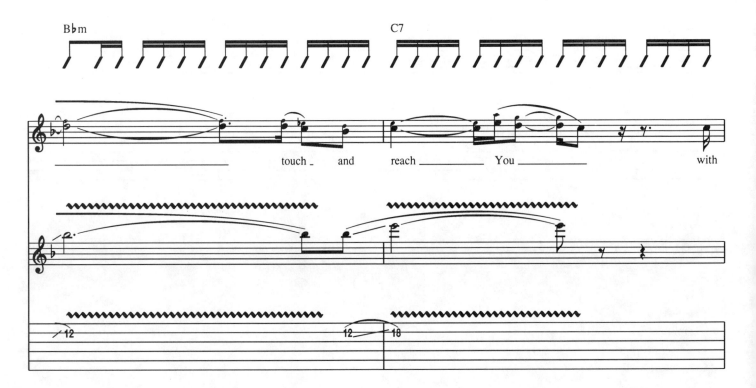

touch and reach You with

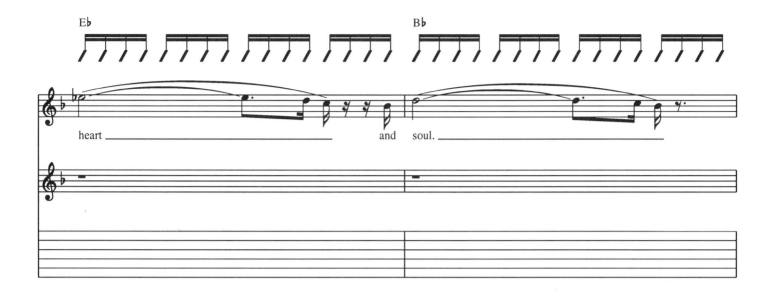

heart _____ and soul.

w/ Rhy. Fig. 2 (Gtr. 1)

Oh, _____ my _____ Lord. _____

w/ Rhy. Fig. 2: Bars 1 - 3 (Gtr. 1)

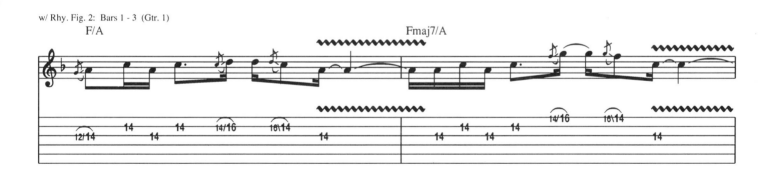

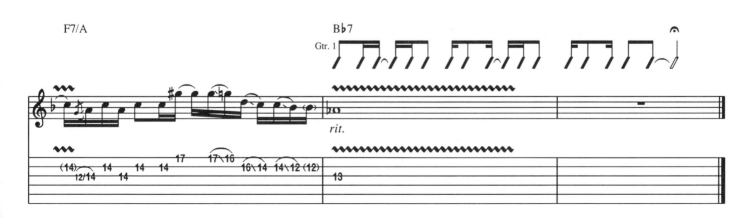

rit.

Here Comes The Sun

By George Harrison

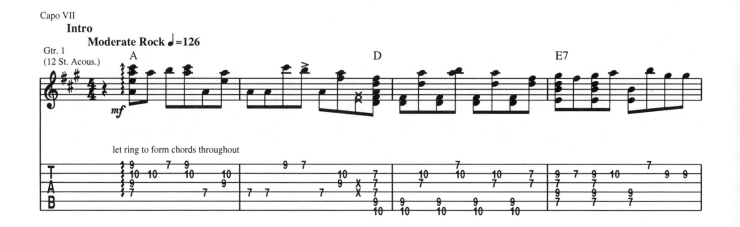

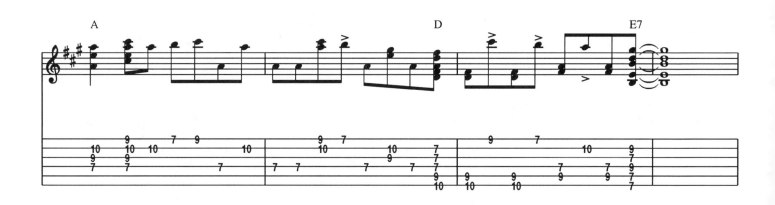

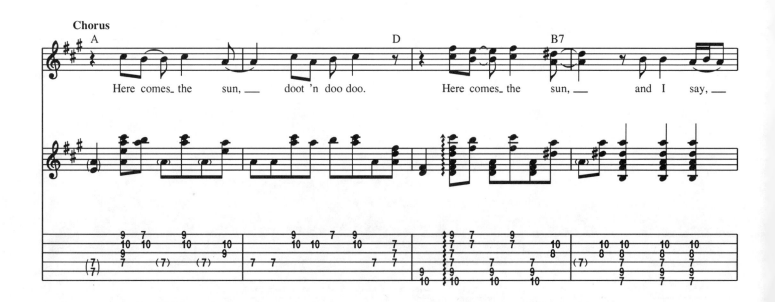

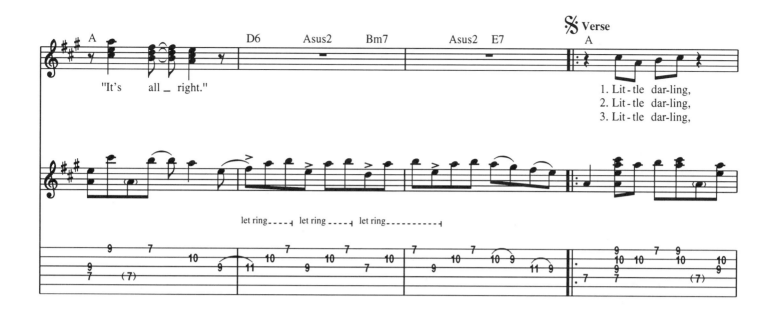

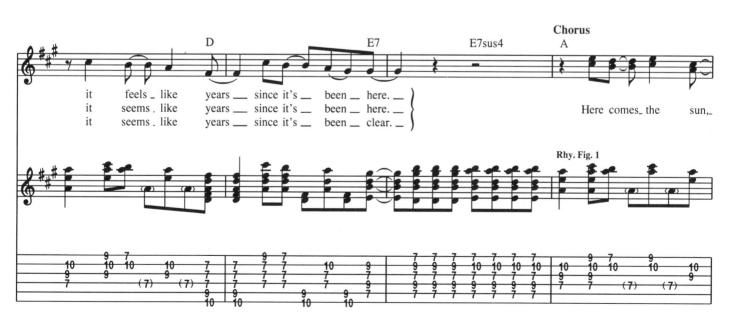

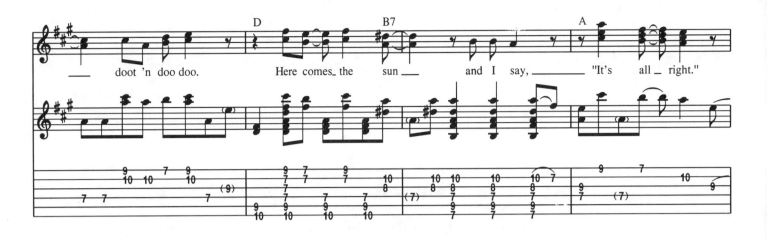

doot 'n doo doo.   Here comes the sun   and I say,   "It's all right."

To Coda ⊕

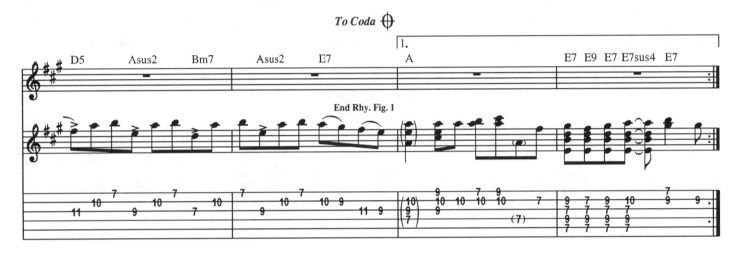

End Rhy. Fig. 1

let ring   let ring   let ring

Bridge

Sun,   sun,   sun,   here it comes.   Sun,

let ring   let ring   let ring   let ring

I Me Mine

By George Harrison

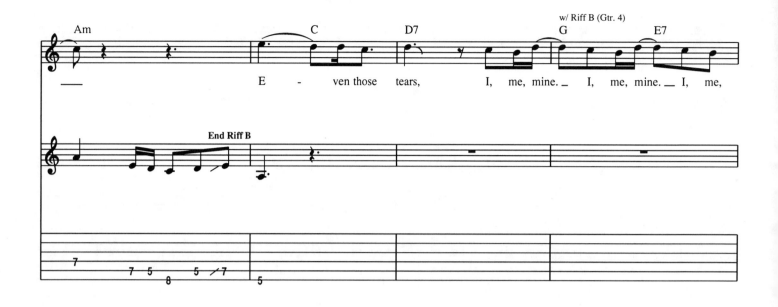

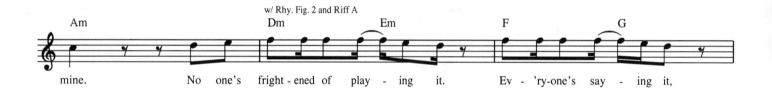

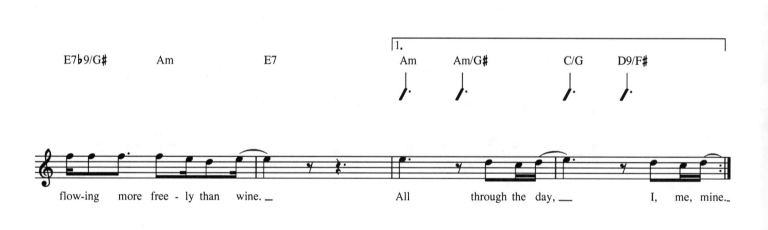

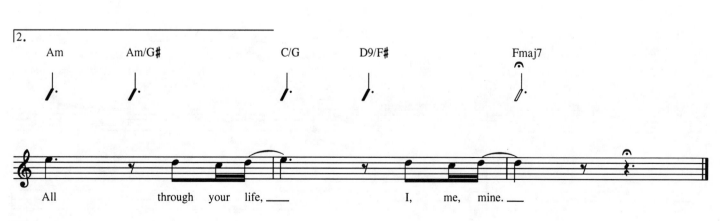

Isn't It A Pity

By George Harrison

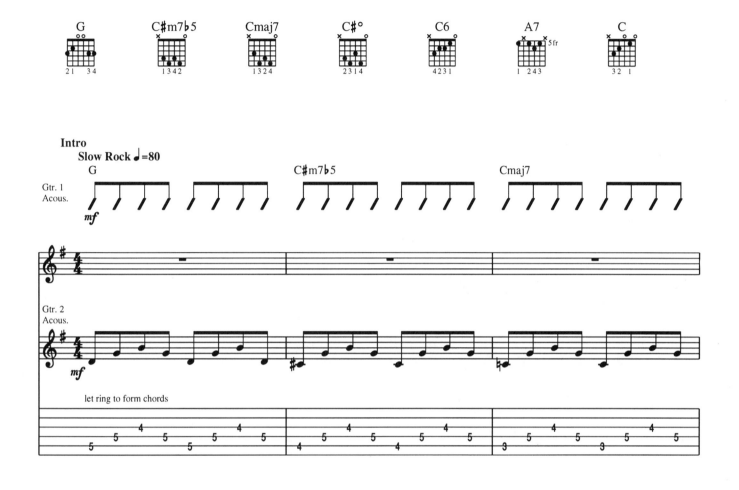

1. Is-n't it ____ a pit - y?
2.,3. *See Additional Lyrics*

w/ Fill 4: 3rd time only (Gtr. 3)

for-get-ting   to give   back.

Isn't   it   a   pit - y?

w/ Rhy. Figs. 1 & 1a,
Bars 9 - 16 (Gtrs. 1 & 2)
Interlude

End Rhy. Fig. 1

End Rhy. Fig. 1a

Gtr. 3

loco

w/ slide

Fill 1
Gtr. 3

Fill 4
Gtr. 3

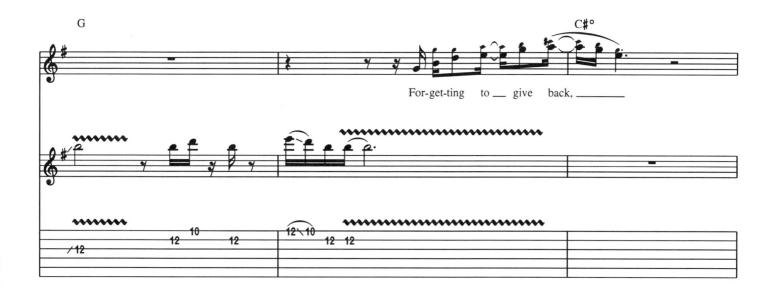

For-get-ting   to __ give   back, _____

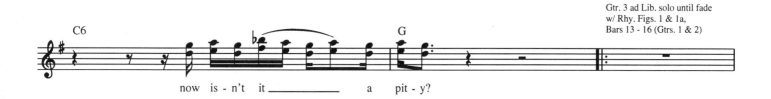

Gtr. 3 ad Lib. solo until fade
w/ Rhy. Figs. 1 & 1a,
Bars 13 - 16 (Gtrs. 1 & 2)

now   is - n't   it _____   a   pit - y?

Repeat and Fade

What   a   pit - y.   What   a   pit - y.

Additional Lyrics

Verse 2

Some things take so long.
But how do I explain
When not too many people
Can see we're all the same.
And because of all their tears,
Their eyes can't hope to see
The beauty that surrounds them.
Isn't it a pity?

Verse 3

Isn't it a pity?
Now isn't it a shame?
How we break each other's hearts
And cause each other pain.
How we take each other's love
Without thinking anymore.
Forgetting to give back,
Isn't it a pity?

My Sweet Lord

By George Harrison

Mmm, _____ my Lord. ___ I real - ly want to

w/ Rhy. Fig. 2
Chorus

see You. Real - ly want to be with You. Real - ly want to
know You. Real - ly want to go with You. Real - ly want to

2nd time only: sing backups

see You Lord, but it takes __ so __ long __ my __ Lord. __ 2. My _____ sweet Lord,
show You Lord, but it won't __ take __ long __ my __ Lord. __ 3. My _____ sweet Lord,
Backups: (Hal - le - lu - jah.)

w/ Rhy. Fig. 1: 3 times (Gtr. 1)
Verse

___ Mmm, __ my __ Lord. ___ My _____ sweet Lord. __
(Hal - le - lu - jah.) (Hal - le - lu - jah.)

Chorus

___ Real - ly want to see You. _ Real - ly want to
(Hal - le - lu - jah.)

Bridge

see You. _ Real - ly want to see _ You Lord. ___ Real - ly want to

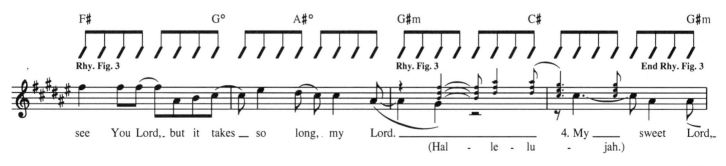

see You Lord, but it takes __ so long, __ my Lord. _____ 4. My __ sweet Lord,
(Hal - le - lu - jah.)

75

5. *See Additional Lyrics for Verse and Backups*

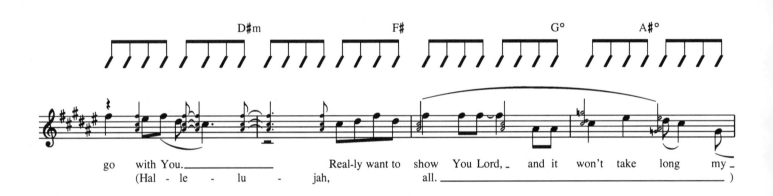

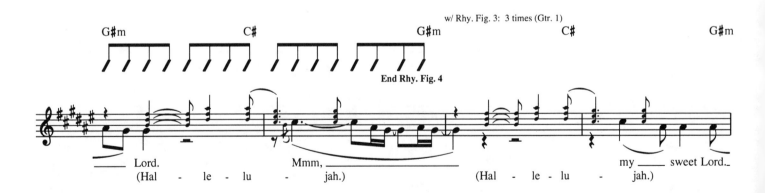

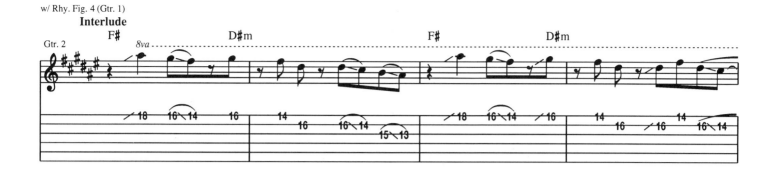

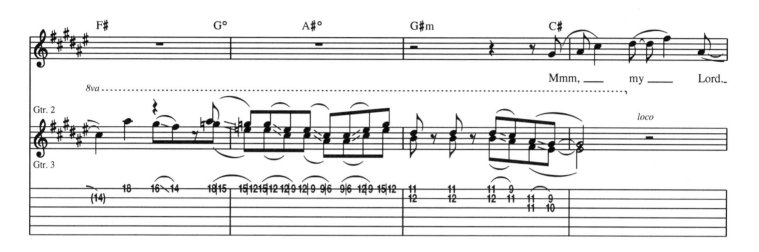

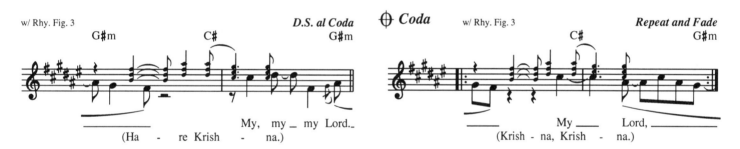

Additional Lyrics

Verse

My Lord, my, my, my Lord.
Oooh.
Now I really want to see You. I really want to be with You.
Really want to see You Lord, but it takes so long my Lord.
My Lord, my, my, my Lord.
My sweet Lord. My sweet Lord.

Backups

Hare Krishna. Hare Krishna.
Krishna, Krishna.
Hare, Hare.
Hare, Rama.
Hare, Rama.
Ahh.
Hallelujah. Hallelujah.
Hare Krishna. Hare Krishna.

Piggies

By George Harrison

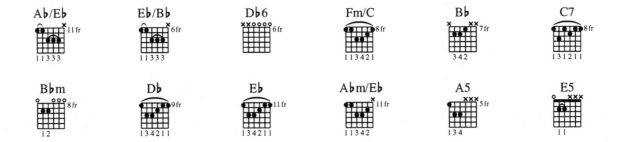

All instruments arr. for gtr.

Capo VI

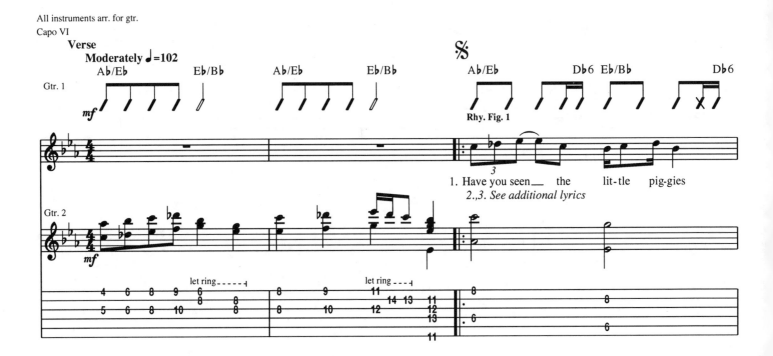

1. Have you seen___ the lit-tle pig-gies
2.,3. *See additional lyrics*

crawl-ing in __ the dirt? And for all __ the lit-tle pig-gies life is get-ting worse,___

In their eyes . there's some-thing lack-ing. What they need's a damn good whack-ing.

w/ Rhy. Fig. 1

Interlude

D.S. al Coda

⊕ *Coda*

Additional Lyrics

Verse 2

Have you seen the little piggies in the starched white shirts?
You will find the bigger piggies stirring up the dirt,
Always have clean shirts to play around in.

Verse 3

Everywhere there's lots of piggies living piggy lives.
You can see them out for dinner with their piggie wives,
Clutching forks and knives to eat their bacon.

Savoy Truffle

Words and Music by George Harrison

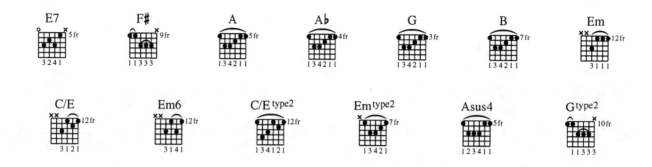

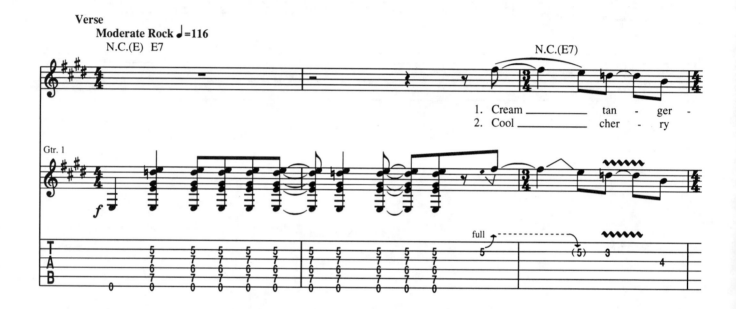

3. Cream . tan - ger-ine and mon-te - li - mar. _

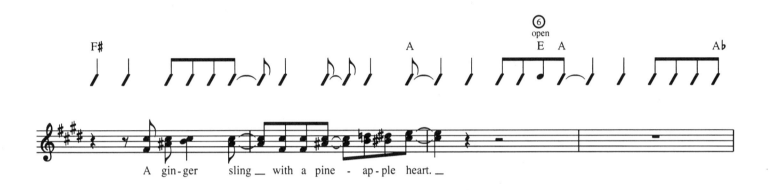

A gin-ger sling _ with a pine - ap-ple heart. _

Cof-fee des - sert, _ yes you know it's good news. _ Whoo. But you'll

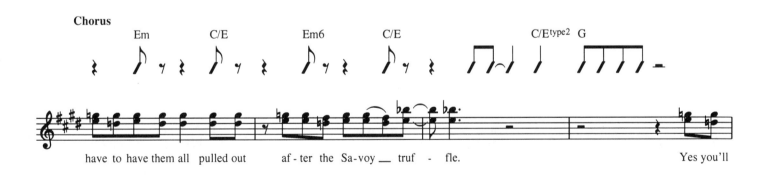

Chorus

have to have them all pulled out af - ter the Sa-voy _ truf - fle. Yes you'll

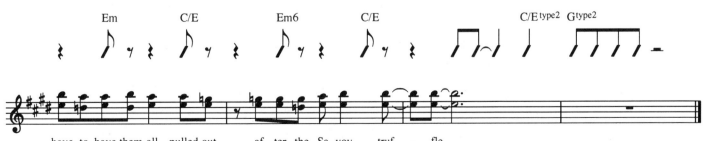

have to have them all pulled out af - ter the Sa-voy truf - fle. _

Something

By George Harrison

* Consider Rhy. Fig. 1 a model for improvisation for 2nd & 3rd verses and gtr. solo

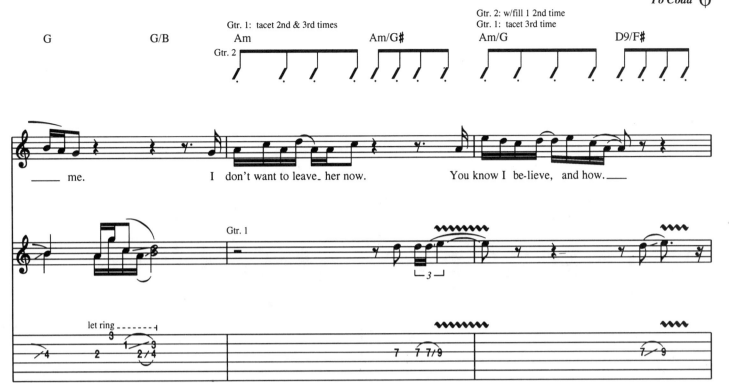

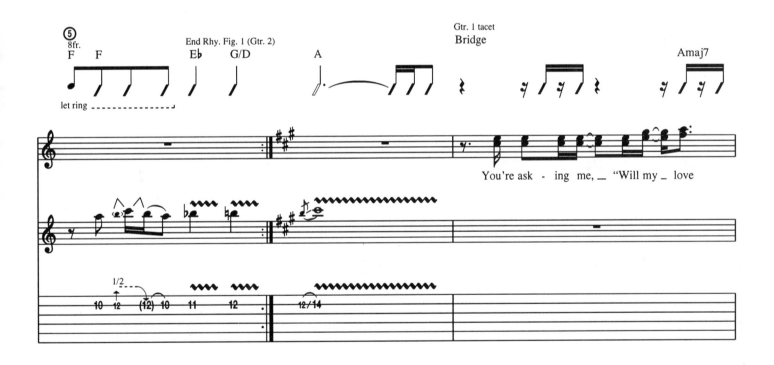

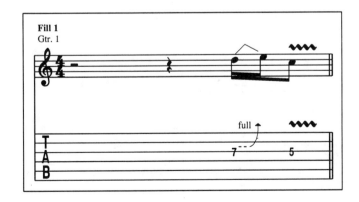

grow?   I don't know. _____ I _____ don't know.

You stick a - round. and it may show.   I don't know. ____ I _____ don't know.

w/ Rhy. Fig. 1

Guitar Solo

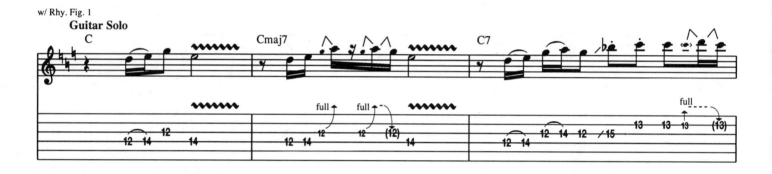

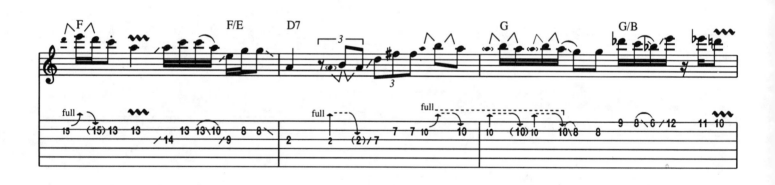

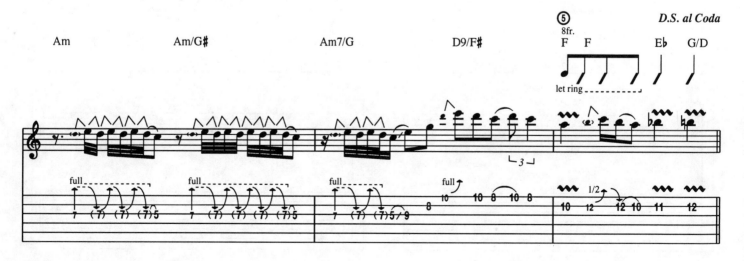

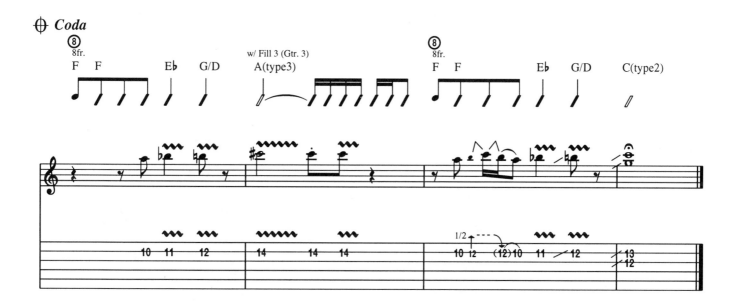

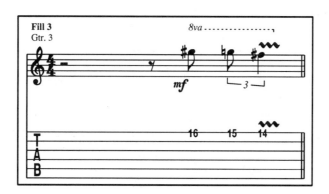

Additional Lyrics

Verse 2

Somewhere in her smile she knows that I don't need no other lover.
Something in her style that shows me.
I don't want to leave her now.
You know I believe and how.

Verse 3

Something in the way she knows and all I have to do is think of her.
Something in the things she shows me.
I don't want to leave her now.
You know I believe and how.

This Song

by George Harrison

song   ain't black or   white   and as far as I   know, ____ don't in-fringe on an - y-one's cop-

- y - right   so... _____   This   song,   we'll __ let   be. -

__ This   song __   is __ in   E. __   This   song __   is __ for __ you. __

To Coda ⊕

End Rhy. Fig. 3

__   and... __

w/ Rhy. Fig. 3 (Gtr. 1)
Saxophone Solo

This

D.C. al Coda

⊕ *Coda*

w/ Rhy. Fig. 2 (Gtr. 1)

Oooh. _____

w/ Rhy. Fig. 3 (Gtr. 1)

Guitar Solo

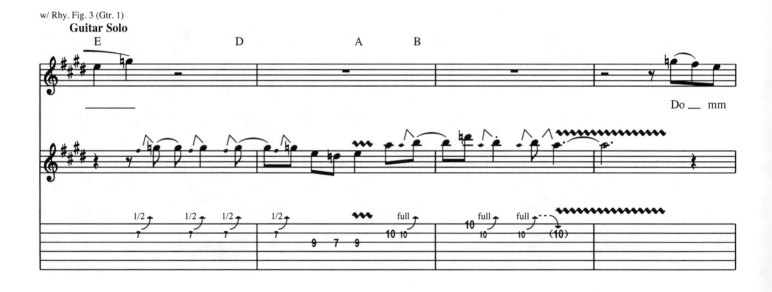

Do __ mm

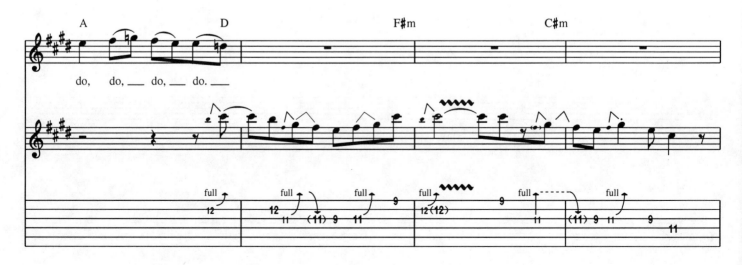

do, do, __ do, __ do. ___

Additional Lyrics

Verse 2

This tune has nothing bright about it.
This tune ain't bad or good
And come ever what may,
My expert tells me it's okay.
As this song came to me
Quite unknowingly,
This song could be you, could be...
Spoken: "Sugar Pie Honey Bunch." No. Sounds more like "Rescue Me."

Verse 3

This riff ain't trying to win gold medals.
This riff ain't hip or square,
Well done or rare,
May end up one more weight to bear.
But this song could well be
A reason to see that
Without you there's no point to this song.

Wah Wah

By George Harrison

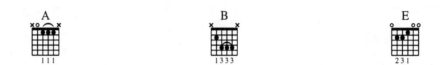

Gtr. 3 open E tuning
④=E ①=E
⑤=A ②=B
⑥=E ③=G#

Intro

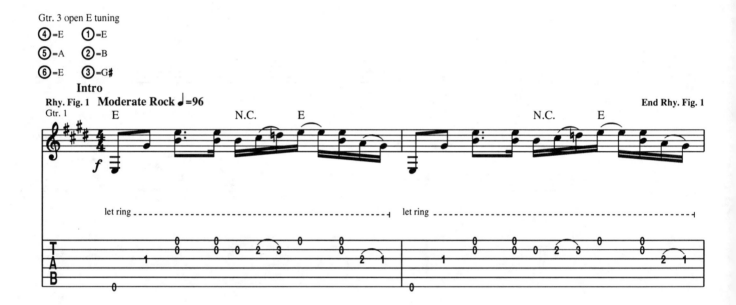

w/ Rhy. Fig. 1 (Gtr. 1)   w/ Rhy. Figs. 1 & 1a (Gtrs. 1 & 2)

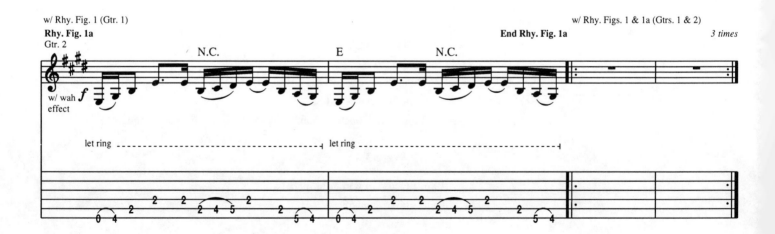

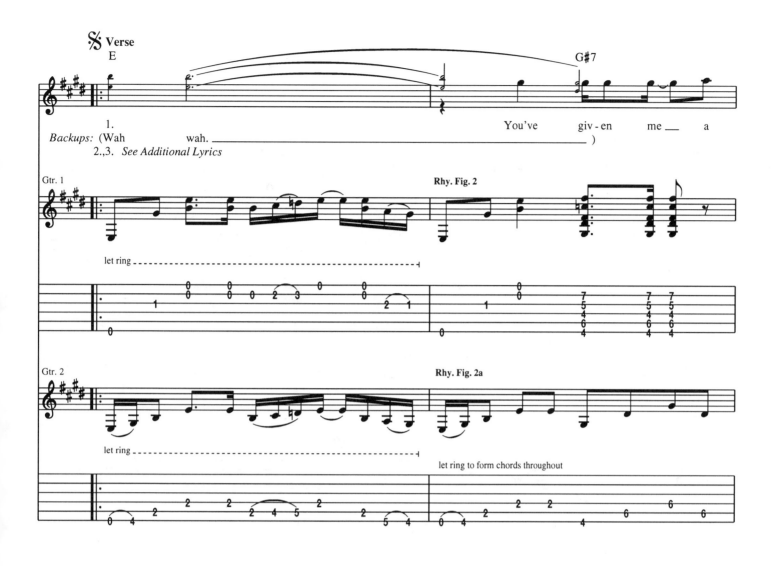

§ **Verse**

1.
Backups: (Wah   wah. _____)
2.,3. *See Additional Lyrics*

You've giv-en me __ a

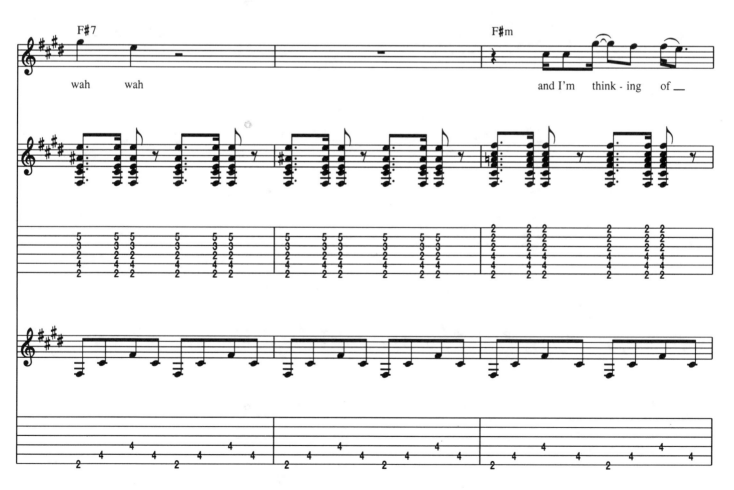

wah   wah   and I'm think-ing of __

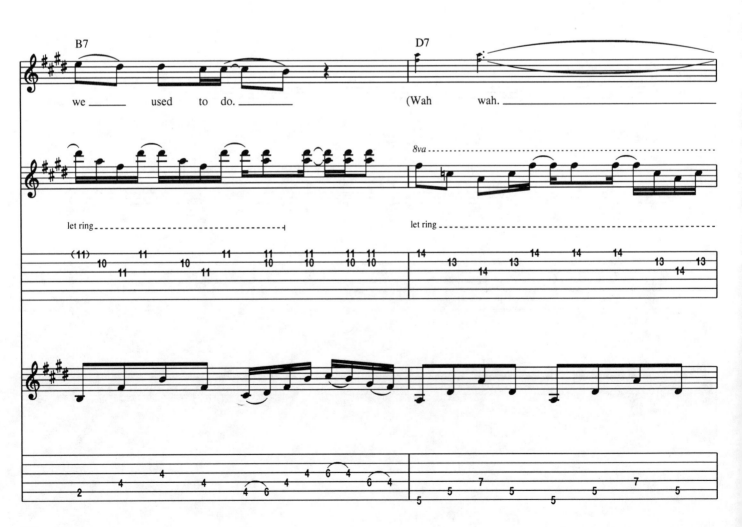

D7#11

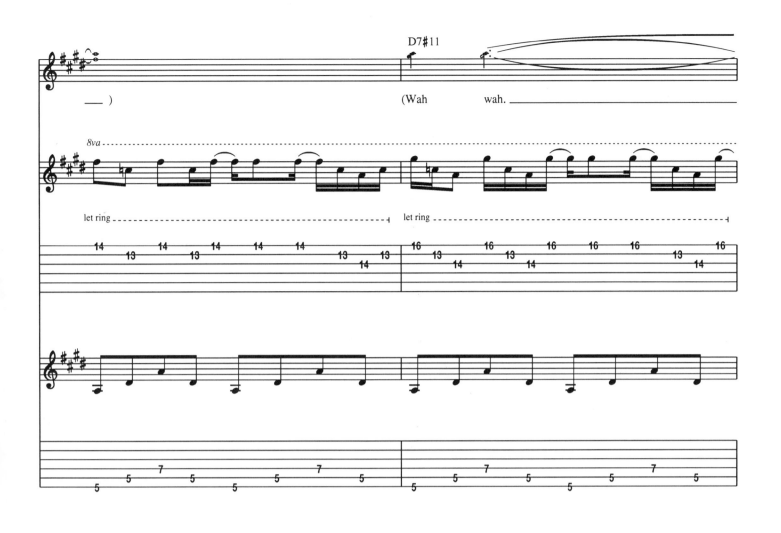

(Wah   wah.

3rd Time: To Coda ⊕

w/ Rhy. Figs. 1 & 1a: 2 times (Gtrs. 1 & 2)

E

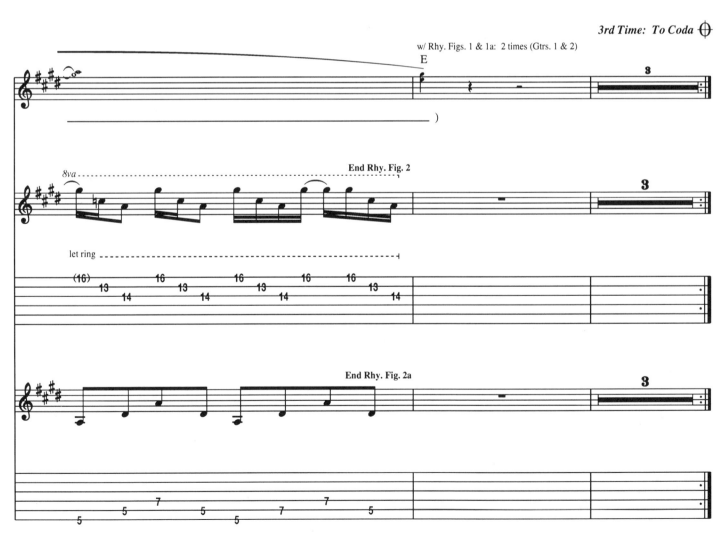

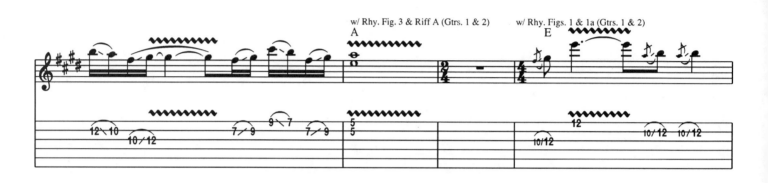

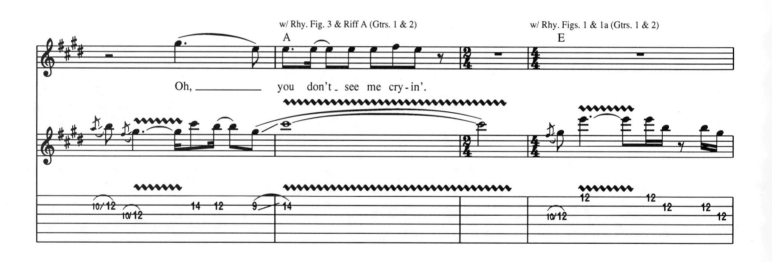

Oh, _____ you don't see me cry-in'.

Oh, _____ you don't hear me sigh-in.'

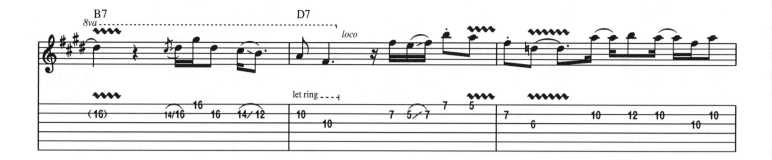

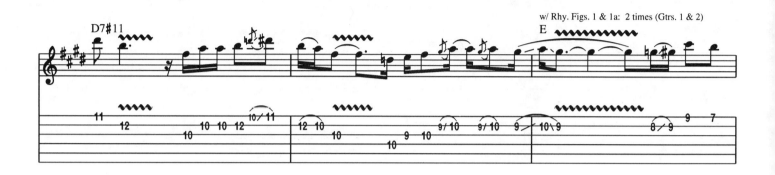

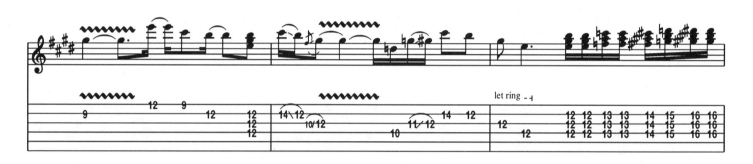

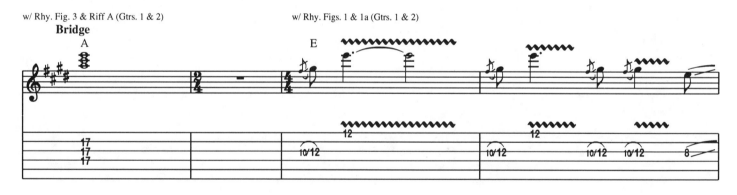

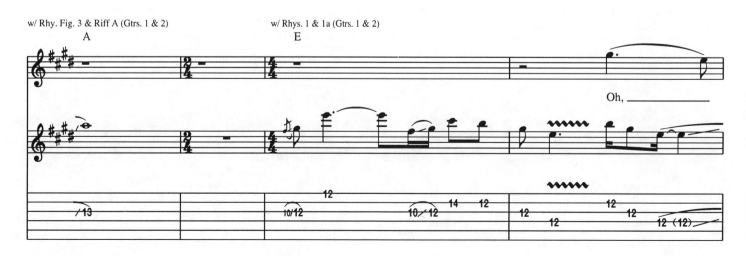

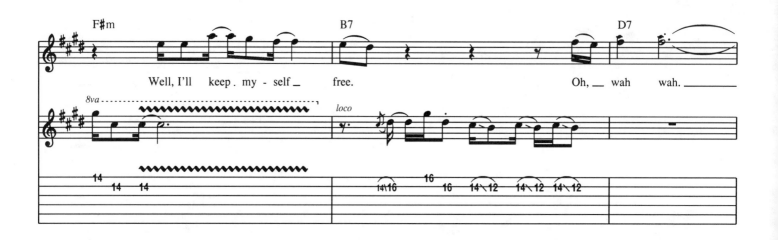

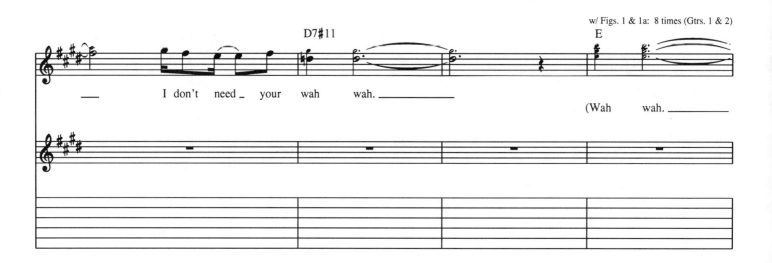

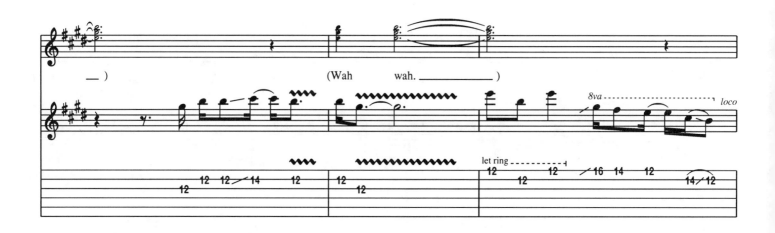

Additional Lyrics

Verse 2

Wah wah.

You made me such a big star.

Being there at the right time

Cheaper than a dime.

Wah wah. You've given me a

Wah wah. Wah wah.

Verse 3

Wah wah.

I don't need no wah wah.

And I know how sweet life can be

If I keep myself free.

Wah wah.

I don't need no wah wah.

Wake Up My Love

By George Harrison

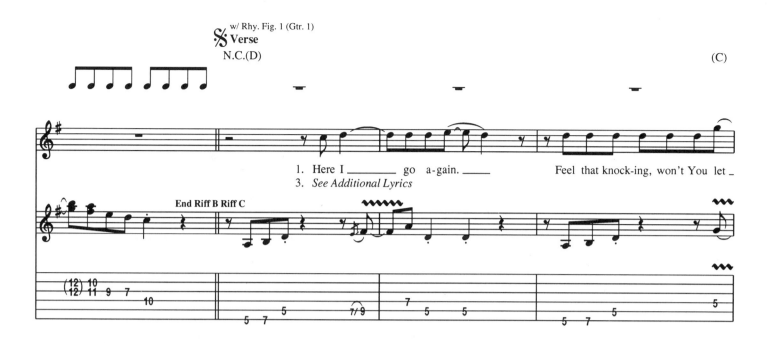

1. Here I _____ go a-gain. _____   Feel that knock-ing, won't You let _
3. *See Additional Lyrics*

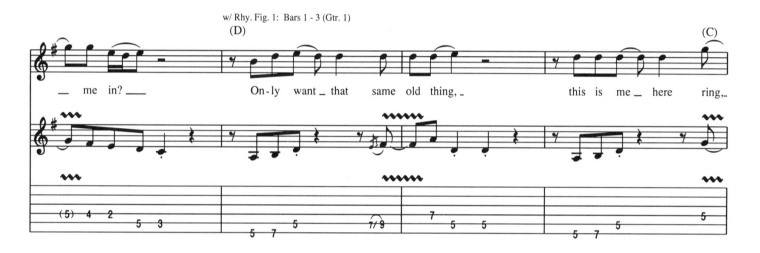

_ me in? ___   On-ly want _ that   same old thing, _   this is me _ here   ring,_

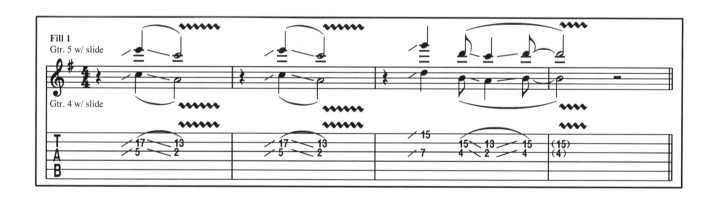

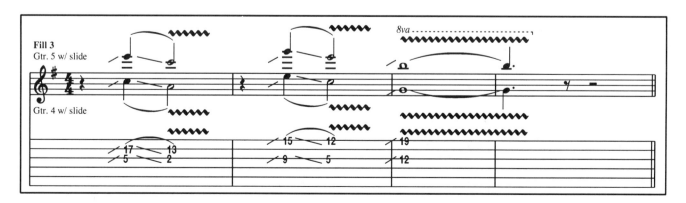

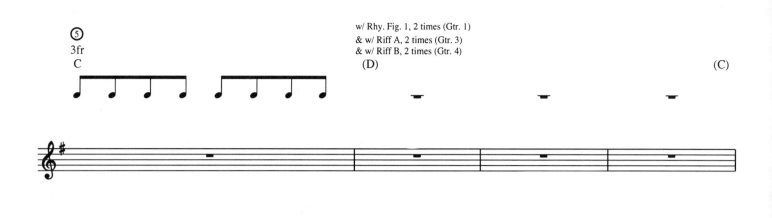

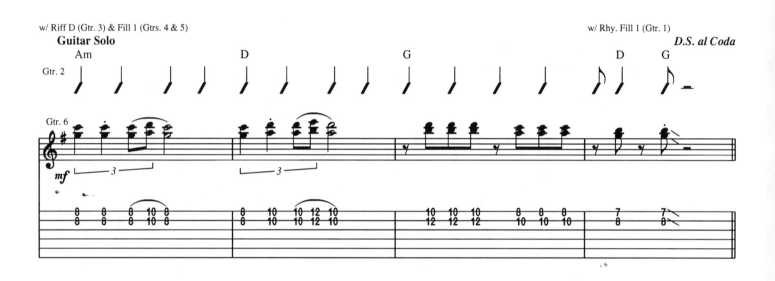

Coda

love.   Wake up, my __ love,   and let it in. __   I want Your

108

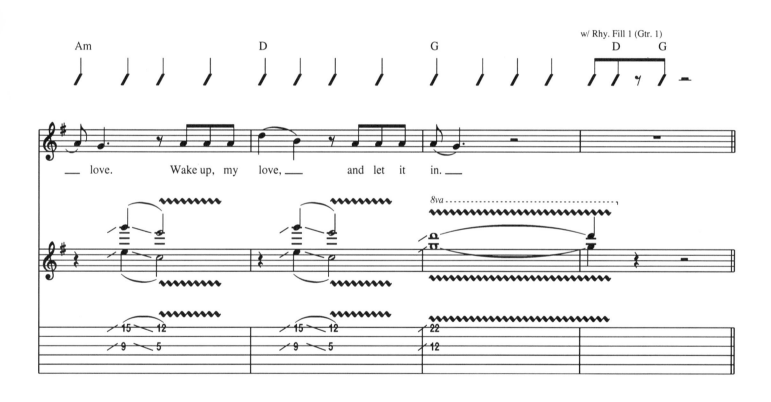

w/ Riff A: 3 times (Gtr. 3)
& Rhy. Fig. 1: 4 times (Gtr. 1)

Verse

I get tired of wrong _ and right. _ You can see _ I need _ Your light. _____

w/ Riff C: Bars 1 - 7 (Gtr. 4)

And that's me knock-ing on Your door. ___ And it's You I'm look - ing for. _____

w/ Rhy. Fig. 1: Bars 1 - 3 (Gtr. 1)

Oh, Lord. _____ Oh, Lord. _____

Gtr. 5 w/ slide

Gtr. 4 w/ slide

w/ Riff E: Bars 1 - 4: 3 times (Gtr. 3)

Chorus

Wake up, my __ love, and let it in. __ I want to

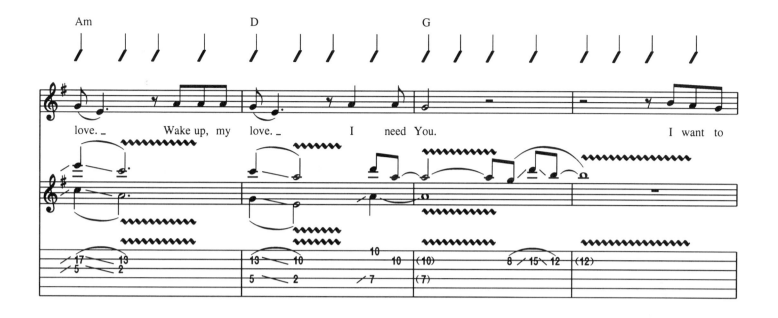

Fade

Additional Lyrics

Verse 3

My life's been so many ways.
Too much darkness gets me crazed.
All around us people fight.
Christ, I'm looking for some light.
Inside Your love.

Verse 4

I don't have no friends of mine
Who can swing me down that vine.
Not much sense in what I do.
That is why I'm calling You. (Inside my...)

What Is Life

By George Harrison

but my love __ is there . for you an - y time __ of day._

w/ Rhy. Fill 1 (Gtr. 2)

w/ Rhy. Fig. 3 & Riff C (Gtrs. 1 & 3)
w/ Rhy. Fig. 3, Riff C & Fill 2: 3rd time (Gtrs. 1, 2 & 3)

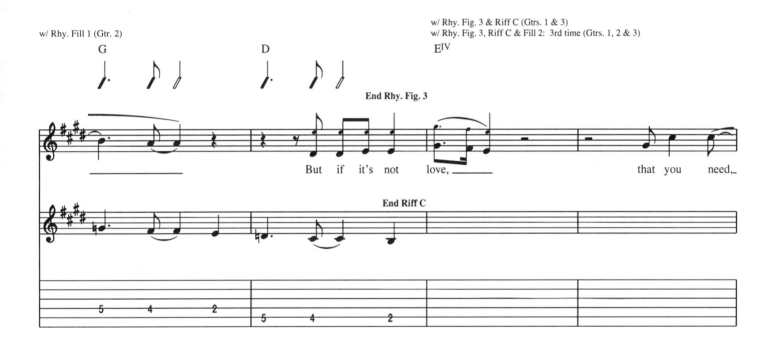

But if it's not love, _____ that you need,_

w/ Fill 3: 3rd time (Gtr. 2)

then I'll try ____ my best __ to make ev - 'ry - thing __ suc - ceed._

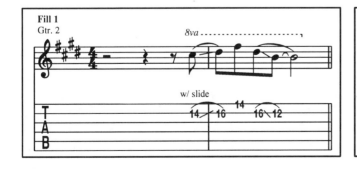

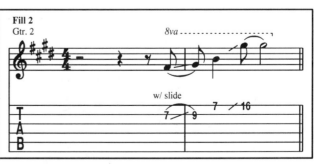

Additional Lyrics

Verse 2

What I know

I can do.

If I give my love, now,

To everyone like you,

But if it's not love

That you need,

Then I'll try my best to make

Everything succeed.

While My Guitar Gently Weeps

By George Harrison

still my gui-tar _____ gen - tly weeps. _____

1. I don't know why _____ no - bod - y told _____ you,
2. I don't know why _____ you _ were di -vert - ed.

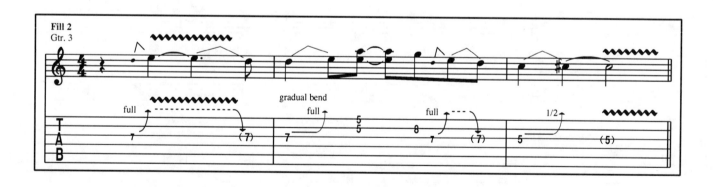

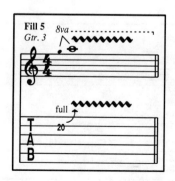

how _ to un - fold _____ your love. _
you _ were per - vert - ed, too. _

I don't know how _____ some - one con - trolled you.
I don't know how _____ you _ were in - vert - ed.

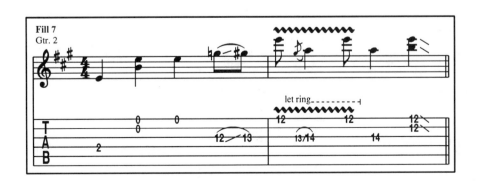

w/ Rhy. Figs. 1 & 2 (Gtrs. 1 & 2)

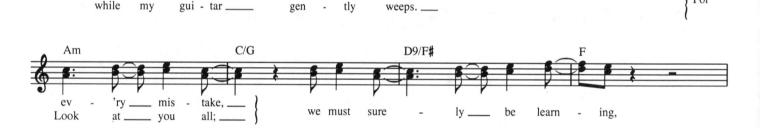

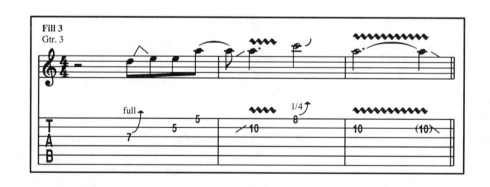

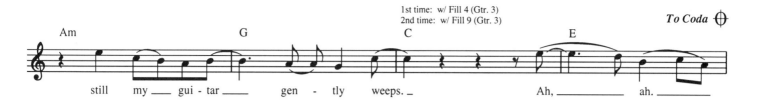

To Coda ⊕

still my ___ gui - tar ___ gen - tly weeps. ___ Ah, ___ ah.

w/ Rhy. Figs. 1 & 2 (Gtrs. 1 & 2)

Guitar Solo

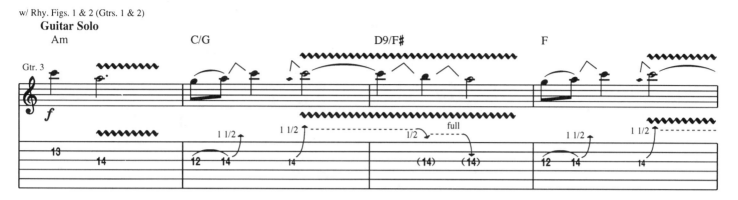

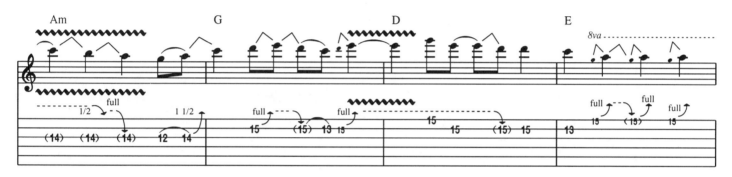

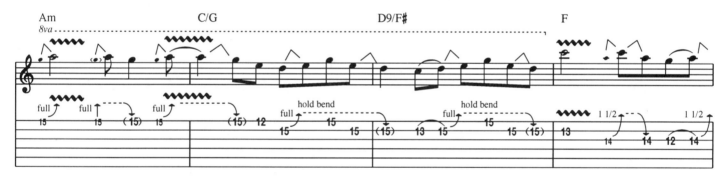

D.S. al Coda

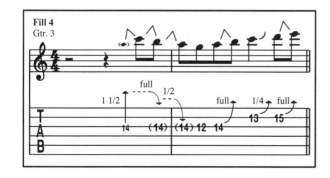

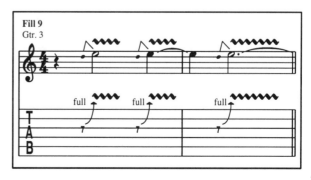

w/ bars 9 - 16 of Rhy. Figs. 1 & 2 (Gtrs. 1 & 2)

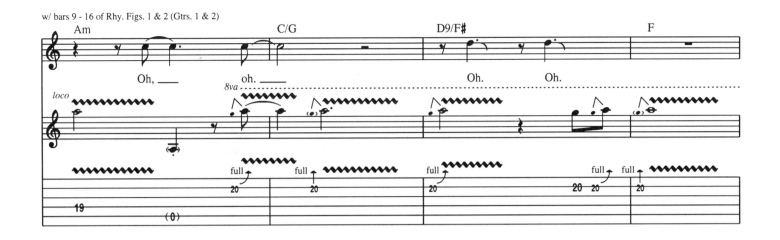

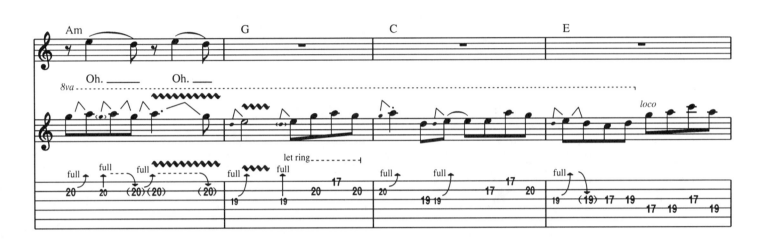

w/ bars 1 - 8 Rhy. Figs. 1 & 2 (Gtrs. 1 & 2)

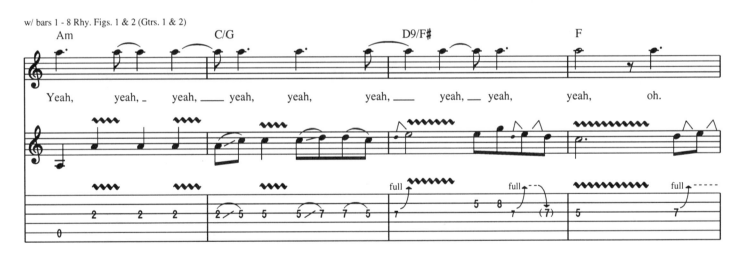

Fade

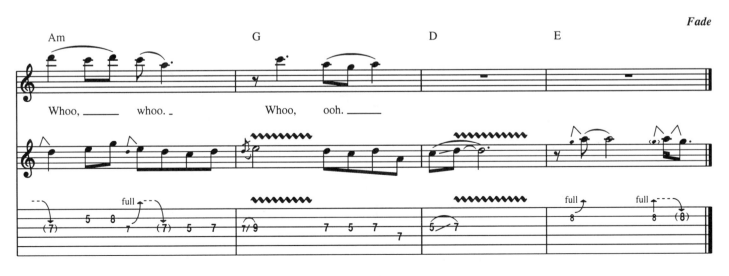

You

By George Harrison

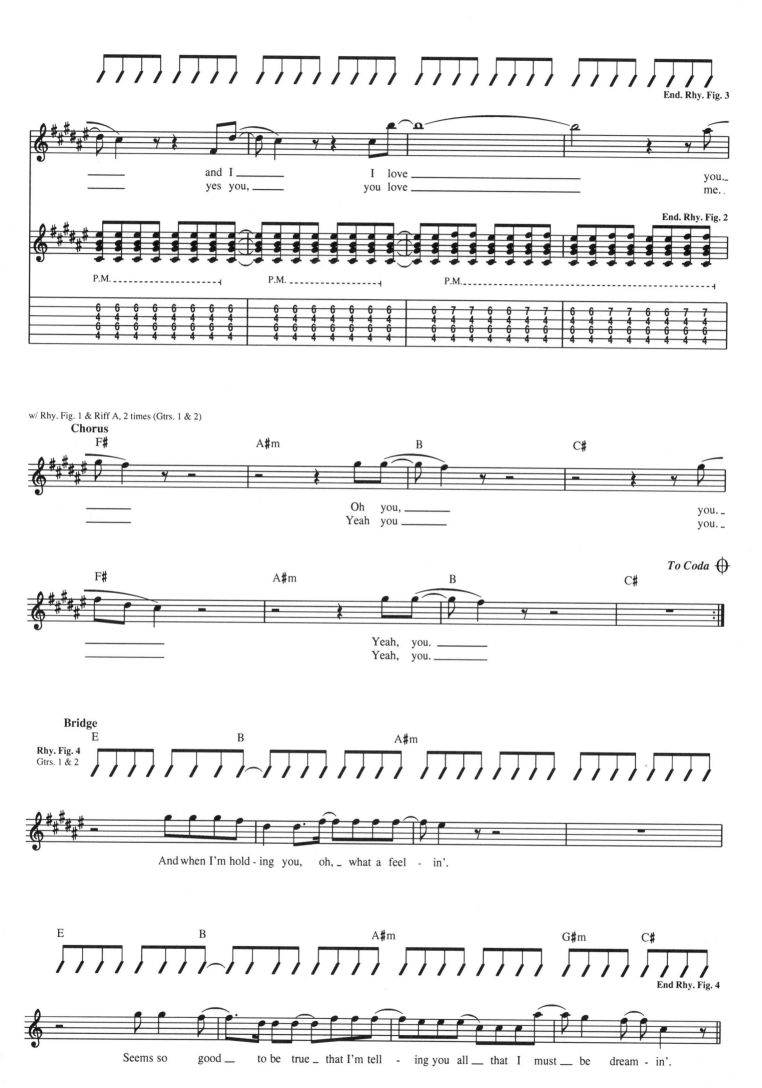

End. Rhy. Fig. 3

and I
yes you,
I love
you love
you.
me.

End. Rhy. Fig. 2

P.M.
P.M.
P.M.

w/ Rhy. Fig. 1 & Riff A, 2 times (Gtrs. 1 & 2)

Chorus

F#   A#m   B   C#

Oh   you,   you.
Yeah you   you.

To Coda ⊕

F#   A#m   B   C#

Yeah, you.
Yeah, you.

Bridge

E   B   A#m

Rhy. Fig. 4
Gtrs. 1 & 2

And when I'm hold - ing you,   oh, _ what a feel - in'.

E   B   A#m   G#m   C#

End Rhy. Fig. 4

Seems so   good _   to be true _ that I'm tell - ing you all _ that I must _ be   dream - in'.

w/ Rhy. Fig. 1 & Riff A for 7 bars (Gtrs. 1 & 2)

Saxophone Solo

And I, ___

___ and I, ___ I love ___ you. ___

w/ Rhy. Fig. 1 (Gtr. 2) & Riff A for 7 bars (Gtr. 1)

Chorus

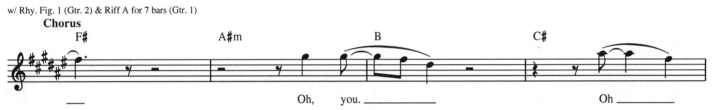

___ Oh, you. ___ Oh ___

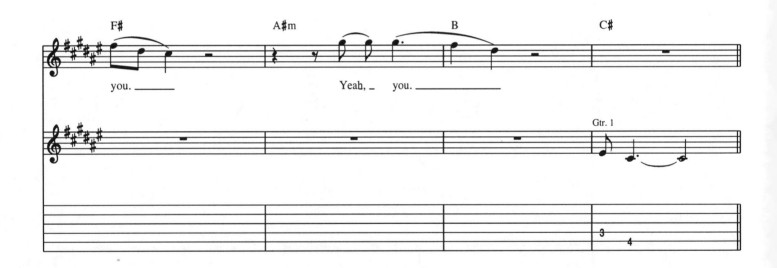

you. ___ Yeah, ___ you. ___

w/ Rhy. Fig. 4 (Gtr. 2)   w/ Rhy. Fig. 4 for bars 2 - 8 (Gtr. 1)

Bridge

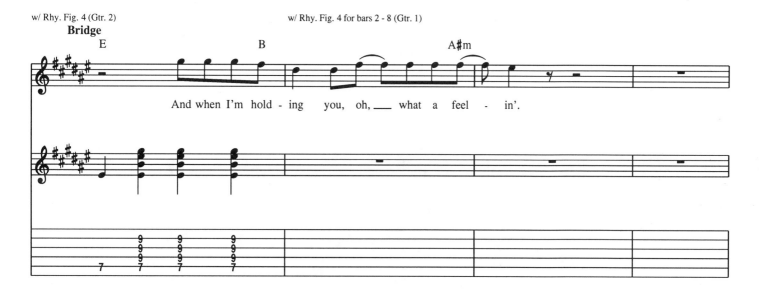

And when I'm hold - ing you, oh, ___ what a feel - in'.

D.S. al Coda

Seems so good ___ to be true, _ that I'm tell - ing you all ___ that I must ___ be dream - in'. I ___

⊕ *Coda*

w/ Rhy. Fig 1 & Riff A, 3 times

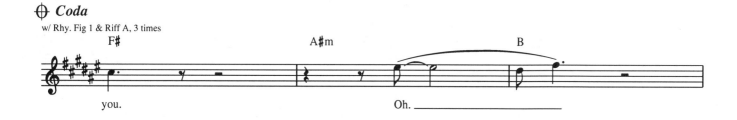

you.   Oh. _____

You know that I love ___ you.   Oh. _____   Oh. .

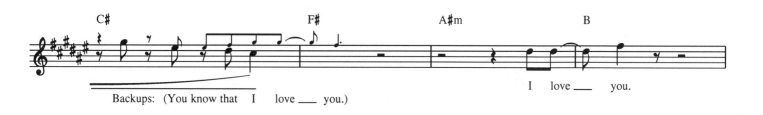

Backups: (You know that I love ___ you.)   I love ___ you.

w/ Rhy. Fig. 1 & Riff A for 3 bars   *Fade*

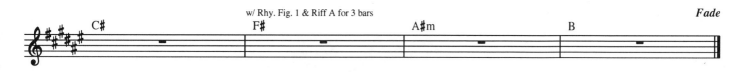

When We Was Fab

Words and Music by Jeff Lynne and George Harrison

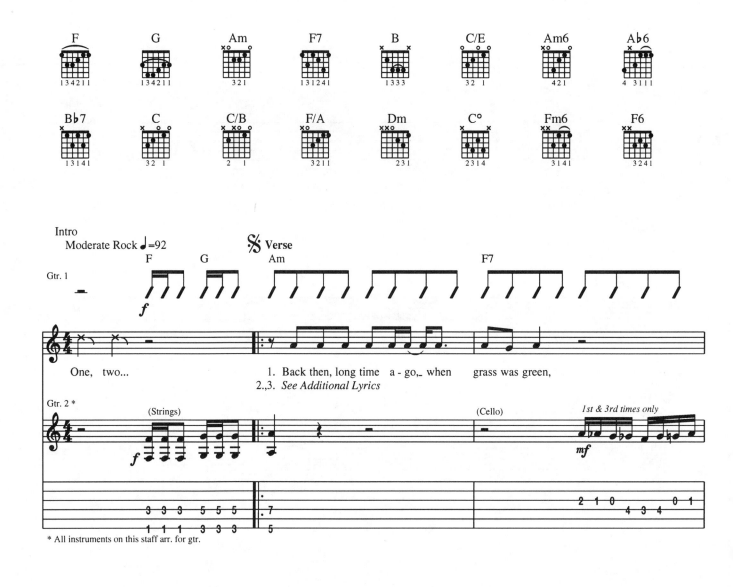

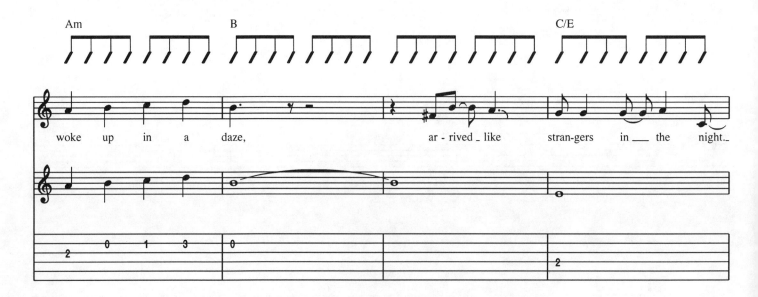

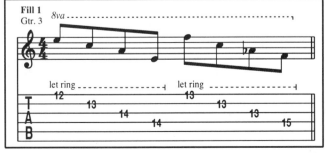

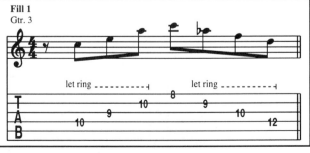

Long time a-go, _ when we was fab.   Fab,   like this pull-o-ver you sent
fab.)   (Ah. _____

to me. _____)   (Oh,   Fab.   Gear!   (Whee!)
do, do do.)

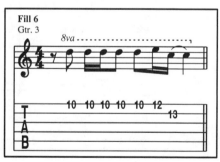

* See preceeding page

* See preceeding page

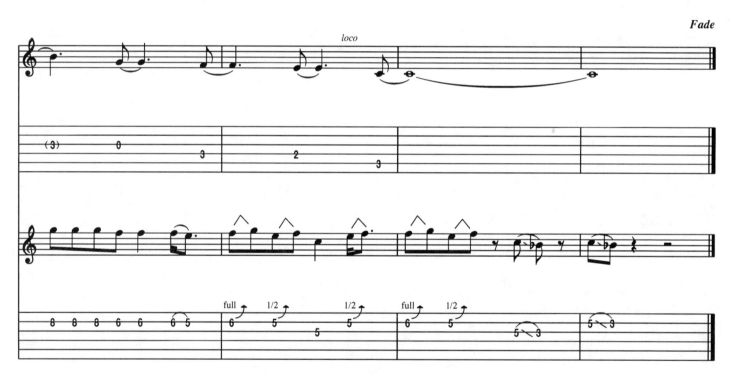

Additional Lyrics

Verse 2

Caressers fleeced you in the morning light.
Casualties at dawn,
And we did it all.

Verse 3

The microscopes that magnified the tears
Studied warts and all.
Still the life flowed on and on.

NOTATION LEGEND

RECORDED VERSIONS
The Best Note-For-Note Transcriptions Available

RECORDED VERSIONS GUITAR®

ALL BOOKS INCLUDE TABLATURE

00690501	Adams, Bryan – Greatest Hits $19.95
00692015	Aerosmith – Greatest Hits $22.95
00690488	Aerosmith – Just Push Play $19.95
00690178	Alice in Chains – Acoustic $19.95
00694865	Alice in Chains – Dirt $19.95
00694925	Alice in Chains – Jar of Flies/Sap $19.95
00690387	Alice in Chains – Nothing Safe –
	The Best of the Box $19.95
00694932	Allman Brothers Band – Volume 1 ....$24.95
00694933	Allman Brothers Band – Volume 2 ....$24.95
00694934	Allman Brothers Band – Volume 3 ....$24.95
00690513	American Hi-Fi $19.95
00694878	Atkins, Chet – Vintage Fingerstyle $19.95
00690418	Audio Adrenaline, Best of $17.95
00690366	Bad Company Original Anthology - Bk 1 .$19.95
00690367	Bad Company Original Anthology - Bk 2 .$19.95
00694929	Beatles: 1962-1966 ....$24.95
00694930	Beatles: 1967-1970 ....$24.95
00694880	Beatles – Abbey Road $19.95
00690110	Beatles – Book 1 (White Album) $19.95
00694832	Beatles – For Acoustic Guitar $19.95
00660140	Beatles – Guitar Book $19.95
00694863	Beatles –
	Sgt. Pepper's Lonely Hearts Club Band ..$19.95
00690397	Beck – Midnite Vultures $19.95
00694884	Benson, George – Best of $19.95
00692385	Berry, Chuck $19.95
00692200	Black Sabbath –
	We Sold Our Soul for Rock 'N' Roll $19.95
00690305	Blink 182 – Dude Ranch $19.95
00690389	Blink 182 – Enema of the State $19.95
00690523	Blink 182 – Take Off Your Pants & Jacket .$19.95
00690028	Blue Oyster Cult – Cult Classics $19.95
00690168	Buchanan, Roy – Collection $19.95
00690491	Bowie, David – Best of $19.95
00690451	Buckley, Jeff – Collection $24.95
00690364	Cake – Songbook $19.95
00690293	Chapman, Steven Curtis – Best of $19.95
00690043	Cheap Trick – Best of $19.95
00690171	Chicago – Definitive Guitar Collection ...$22.95
00690415	Clapton Chronicles – Best of Eric Clapton .$18.95
00690393	Clapton, Eric – Selections from Blues $19.95
00690074	Clapton, Eric – The Cream of Clapton ...$24.95
00690010	Clapton, Eric – From the Cradle $19.95
00660139	Clapton, Eric – Journeyman $19.95
00694869	Clapton, Eric – Unplugged $22.95
00694896	Clapton, Eric/John Mayall – Bluesbreakers .$19.95
00690162	Clash, Best of $19.95
00690494	Coldplay – Parachutes $19.95
00694940	Counting Crows – August & Everything After .$19.95
00694840	Cream – Disraeli Gears $19.95
00690401	Creed – Human Clay $19.95
00690352	Creed – My Own Prison $19.95
00690484	dc Talk – Intermission: The Greatest Hits .$19.95
00690289	Deep Purple, Best of $17.95
00690384	Di Franco, Ani – Best of $19.95
00690322	Di Franco, Ani – Little Plastic Castle ...$19.95
00690380	Di Franco, Ani – Up Up Up Up Up Up ...$19.95
00695382	Dire Straits – Sultans of Swing $19.95
00690347	Doors, The – Anthology $22.95
00690348	Doors, The – Essential Guitar Collection .$16.95
00690524	Etheridge, Melissa – Skin $19.95
00690349	Eve 6 ....$19.95
00690496	Everclear, Best of $19.95
00690515	Extreme II – Pornograffitti $19.95
00690323	Fastball – All the Pain Money Can Buy ..$19.95
00690235	Foo Fighters – The Colour and the Shape .$19.95

00690394	Foo Fighters –
	There Is Nothing Left to Lose $19.95
00690222	G3 Live – Satriani, Vai, Johnson $22.95
00690536	Garbage – Beautiful Garbage $19.95
00690438	Genesis Guitar Anthology $19.95
00690338	Goo Goo Dolls – Dizzy Up the Girl $19.95
00690114	Guy, Buddy – Collection Vol. A-J $22.95
00690193	Guy, Buddy – Collection Vol. L-Y $22.95
00694798	Harrison, George – Anthology $19.95
00692930	Hendrix, Jimi – Are You Experienced? ...$24.95
00692931	Hendrix, Jimi – Axis: Bold As Love $22.95
00694944	Hendrix, Jimi – Blues $24.95
00692932	Hendrix, Jimi – Electric Ladyland $24.95
00690218	Hendrix, Jimi – First Rays of the New Rising Sun $27.95
00690017	Hendrix, Jimi – Woodstock $24.95
00660029	Holly, Buddy $19.95
00690054	Hootie & The Blowfish –
	Cracked Rear View $19.95
00690457	Incubus – Make Yourself $19.95
00690544	Incubus – Morningview $19.95
00690136	Indigo Girls – 1200 Curfews $22.95
00694833	Joel, Billy – For Guitar $19.95
00694912	Johnson, Eric – Ah Via Musicom $19.95
00694799	Johnson, Robert – At the Crossroads $19.95
00690271	Johnson, Robert – The New Transcriptions $24.95
00699131	Joplin, Janis – Best of $19.95
00693185	Judas Priest – Vintage Hits $19.95
00690444	King, B.B. and Eric Clapton –
	Riding with the King $19.95
00690339	Kinks, The – Best of $19.95
00690279	Liebert, Ottmar + Luna Negra –
	Opium Highlights $19.95
00694755	Malmsteen, Yngwie – Rising Force $19.95
00694956	Marley, Bob – Legend $19.95
00694945	Marley, Bob – Songs of Freedom $24.95
00690283	McLachlan, Sarah – Best of $19.95
00690382	McLachlan, Sarah – Mirrorball $19.95
00690442	Matchbox 20 – Mad Season $19.95
00690239	Matchbox 20 – Yourself or Someone Like You .$19.95
00694952	Megadeth – Countdown to Extinction ...$19.95
00690391	Megadeth – Risk $19.95
00694951	Megadeth – Rust in Peace $22.95
00690495	Megadeth – The World Needs a Hero $19.95
00690040	Miller, Steve, Band – Greatest Hits $19.95
00690448	MxPx – The Ever Passing Moment $19.95
00690189	Nirvana – From the Muddy
	Banks of the Wishkah $19.95
00694913	Nirvana – In Utero $19.95
00694883	Nirvana – Nevermind $19.95
00690026	Nirvana – Unplugged™ in New York $19.95
00690121	Oasis – (What's the Story) Morning Glory .$19.95
00690358	Offspring, The – Americana $19.95
00690485	Offspring, The – Conspiracy of One $19.95
00690203	Offspring, The – Smash $18.95
00694847	Osbourne, Ozzy – Best of $22.95
00694830	Osbourne, Ozzy – No More Tears $19.95
00690538	Oysterhead – The Grand Pecking Order ...$19.95
00694865	Pearl Jam – Ten $19.95
00690439	Perfect Circle, A – Mer De Noms $19.95
00690176	Phish – Billy Breathes $22.95
00690424	Phish – Farmhouse $19.95
00690240	Phish – Hoist $19.95
00690331	Phish – Story of the Ghost $19.95
00690428	Pink Floyd – Dark Side of the Moon $19.95
00690456	P.O.D. – The Fundamental
	Elements of Southtown $19.95
00693864	Police, The – Best of $19.95

00690299	Presley, Elvis – Best of Elvis:
	The King of Rock 'n' Roll $19.9
00694975	Queen – Greatest Hits $24.9
00694910	Rage Against the Machine $19.9
00690395	Rage Against the Machine –
	The Battle of Los Angeles $19.9
00690145	Rage Against the Machine – Evil Empire .$19.9
00690478	Rage Against the Machine – Renegades ..$19.9
00690426	Ratt – Best of $19.9
00690055	Red Hot Chili Peppers –
	Bloodsugarsexmagik $19.9
00690379	Red Hot Chili Peppers – Californication ..$19.9
00690090	Red Hot Chili Peppers – One Hot Minute .$22.9
00694899	R.E.M. – Automatic for the People $19.9
00690014	Rolling Stones – Exile on Main Street $24.9
00690135	Rush, Otis – Collection $19.9
00690502	Saliva – Every Six Seconds $19.9
00690031	Santana's Greatest Hits $19.9
00120123	Shepherd, Kenny Wayne – Trouble Is ...$19.9
00690419	Slipknot $19.9
00690530	Slipknot – Iowa $19.9
00690330	Social Distortion – Live at the Roxy $19.9
00690385	Sonicflood $19.9
00694957	Stewart, Rod – Unplugged...And Seated ..$22.9
00690021	Sting – Fields of Gold $19.9
00690519	Sum 41 – All Killer No Filler $19.9
00690425	System of a Down $19.9
00690531	System of a Down – Toxicity $19.9
00694824	Taylor, James – Best of $16.9
00690238	Third Eye Blind $19.9
00690403	Third Eye Blind – Blue $19.9
00690295	Tool – Aenima $19.9
00690039	Vai, Steve – Alien Love Secrets $24.9
00690343	Vai, Steve – Flex-able Leftovers $19.9
00660137	Vai, Steve – Passion & Warfare $24.9
00690392	Vai, Steve – The Ultra Zone $19.9
00690370	Vaughan, Stevie Ray and Double Trouble –
	The Real Deal: Greatest Hits Volume 2 ..$22.9
00690455	Vaughan, Stevie Ray – Blues at Sunrise ...$19.9
00690116	Vaughan, Stevie Ray – Guitar Collection ...$24.9
00660136	Vaughan, Stevie Ray – In Step $19.9
00660058	Vaughan, Stevie Ray –
	Lightnin' Blues 1983-1987 ....$24.9
00690417	Vaughan, Stevie Ray – Live at Carnegie Hall $19.9
00694835	Vaughan, Stevie Ray – The Sky Is Crying .$22.9
00690015	Vaughan, Stevie Ray – Texas Flood $19.9
00120026	Walsh, Joe – Look What I Did... ......$24.9
00694789	Waters, Muddy – Deep Blues $24.9
00690071	Weezer $19.9
00690516	Weezer (The Green Album) $19.9
00690286	Weezer – Pinkerton $19.9
00690447	Who, The – Best of $24.9
00690320	Williams, Dar – Best of $17.9
00690319	Wonder, Stevie – Some of the Best $17.9
00690443	Zappa, Frank – Hot Rats $19.9